It's About Life

Also by Hyatt Moore

Pass the Word
Any Given Day in the Life of the Bible
The Alphabet Makers
In the Image of God, Faces and Souls that Reflect their Creator
In Search of the Source (with Neil Anderson)

It's About Life

A Philosophical Reverie Pointing to the Source of All

Hyatt Moore

Moore & Moore Art, Dana Point, California

Published by Moore & Moore Art
Dana Point, California
Printed in the U.S.A.

All artwork by the author.

The contents of this book were first published in blog form.
To read current blogs, or to subscribe, go to www.hyattmoore.com, "Blank Slate."

This book is available at www.amazon.com, and at www.hyattmoore.com.

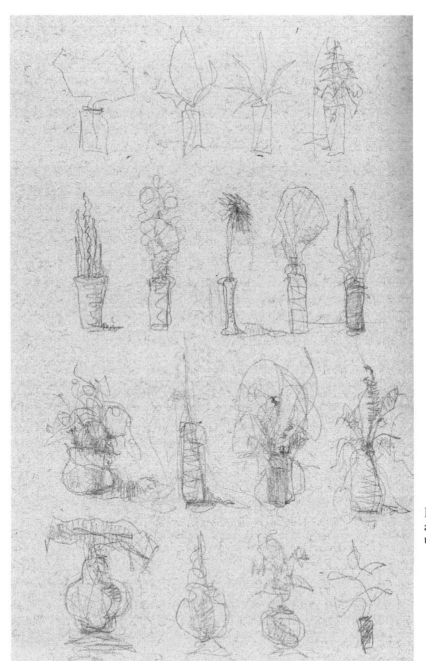

For my children,
and theirs, each
unique.

LIMA AIRPORT 10/24/96

Here, as with most sketches in the book, is a scene not static. One learns to draw fast. When subjects move away, or my time's up, the drawing's done. Life moves on.

Introduction

Ecclesiastes is my favorite book. At least it's up there with my top 66. The fact that it starts out with everything being meaningless doesn't bother me much, particularly when in the end, it says the opposite.

The word "meaningless" is really better translated "vapor." And vapor turns back into rain, which waters the earth. I'm wonderfully watered by the words in that book.

It's a book that seems esoteric at times, inscrutable, and positively negative! But it faces life as it is. I can trust a God that includes in His book the admission that things don't always go as we think they should, that a lot of life is hard to fathom.

In Ecclesiastes I find a thought process that many of us have traveled, questioning the ultimate meaning of everything and ending up empty.

There was a time when I concluded that a pessimist is just a realist who is honest.

Ecclesiastes was written from the perspective of a person who has tried everything, attained everything, and then reflected on it. He never claims to be King Solomon, and the writing style is that of a later usage than Solomon's era. The writer, *Qoheleth*, (the Preacher) has taken on a Solomonic perspective and has written as if he were Solomon.

Since none of us will experience as much as Solomon, the writer gives us the benefit of the conclusion Solomon would have reached if he'd thought on it as much as Qoheleth.

And that is: When all is said and done, all is meaningless—unless and until greater light is found. Of course, that greater light is God Himself. After that, one may still see the anomalies, but there's plenty of reason to be happy . . . in the basic things.

I find a highly positive thread weaving through it all.

So, another book on Ecclesiastes? Yes. It's been done before, but then everything's been done before. Just not by me. And my perspective will be different.

The drawings are from my sketchbooks, done in many places over the years, often in meetings, or just watching. As with the words, they serve as more notes on life and an appreciation for all things. I hope Qohelet would agree.

Self portrait, April 2007

It's My Story, Maybe Yours

"Meaningless! Meaningless!" says the Teacher. —Ecc. 1:2

Why do I love Ecclesiastes so much? A lot of reasons. There's great wisdom in it. It aligns with how I see life. It aligns with my own life.

The writer is one blessed with more human gifts, brains, money and glory than anyone could imagine. Yet, in the end, he's just a man needing God.

Rich or poor, it's the same for all of us. It's pretty normal to feel that true happiness is waiting for us with the next thing. If we could just have _____ (fill in blank) then we'd be content. Then we get that thing and the contentment doesn't last. So we try again. And again and again and again.

In Ecclesiastes, the writer got to the top of all this and, with nothing else to get, he looked around and saw just what you'd think, that it was all meaningless.

What was left but CQE&D? (That's cynicism, questioning everything, and despair.)

He's not the only one that's come to this. Like I said, it's my story.

I began to set my goals in early adulthood. I was married, and figured it was time to get serious. I had five goals—a certain car, a certain boat, a certain house, a certain job, and a certain wife. (Okay, I already had the wife.)

To me, most of these were far off and distant, but the pursuit would give me focus for a long time. To my surprise, within a year, I had them all.

And I'd learned a principle: What you aim for, you arrive at.

It's a nice thing to know when you're a young man starting out. Or anytime.

I also learned another principle: Arriving isn't enough.

I was empty.

I appeared happy. I appeared successful. But I knew different. Worse, I was afraid nothing I could do was going to change it.

I could set new goals. But I knew in time I'd only arrive at them; and then where would I be but where I already was?

That's when the CQE&D set in.

Meaningless, meaningless, says the [Ecclesiastes] Teacher, or "Preacher" in the King James. Not that I was listening to any preacher. Such voice I'd long fled—and covered my tracks.

Now I was alone with my success and, like I said, empty.

To give the rest of the story would mean another book. Suffice to say, in time, God entered the picture and showed me what was missing—namely: Him.

What's happened since then would be a third book.

But this is a meditation on the honest perspectives offered in Ecclesiastes, and how they align with our lives—at least with mine.

I can say with the Joni Mitchell song, "I've looked at life from both sides now."

Happily, I'm on the brighter side. And everything is meaningful.

Edinburgh Castle, Scotland. Powerful, majestic . . . and vain.

A One Word Summary

We were in Edinburgh, Scotland. Because of it, I thought I'd say something pertinent to that. And being in Ecclesiastes, I wanted to say something pertinent to that, too.

First, though, I must confess my utter surprise at what I saw . . . and with that, my utter lack of knowledge of what I might see.

It was my first time in Scotland. I'd been told its beauty was legendary, and many told us to see Edinburgh. But nobody told me why.

Sure enough, we drove through majestic countryside occasioned with charming structures and sheep-dotted hillsides. Then we hit Edinburgh and promptly got lost. Before we finally found our destination, we saw a lot of what seemed like a nice but not that extraordinary a city. We checked into our lodgings and ventured out on foot.

We headed toward the castle, thinking that might be quaint. Wow, was I blown over! What we saw was not only magnificent; it was over-the-top colossal, huge, spread out, and full of history. And the whole area was full of people. Tourists from everywhere crowded the streets. It was another message to me about how little I knew that others apparently did!

In the end, it was my own naiveté that struck me as the thing most amazing.

To take in as much as we could in our limited time, we hopped on a tour bus. Double decker, with guide, and in English (well, Scottish). My amazement continued, now with how much history has taken place in these precincts and, again, by how little I knew of it. And I love history!

It was a great day of taking in sights, marveling, hearing about all the exploits that had gone before, both wise and foolish. But what to equate it with in terms of Ecclesiastes?

"Vanity, vanity," says the Preacher, "All is vanity."

Sorry. That's all that came to mind. It's a summary of the human state, previously and presently. But I must confess, I love it all. Don't know what that says about me, but the next day we went back for more. After that I got a book. There's so much vanity to know!

Cycles and Variations on a Theme

Round and round it goes, ever returning on its course. —Ecc. 1:4-7

Generations come and generations go,
*   but the earth remains forever.*
The sun rises and the sun sets,
*   and hurries back to where it rises.*
The wind blows to the south
*   and turns to the north;*
round and round it goes,
*   ever returning on its course.*
All streams flow into the sea,
*   yet the sea is never full.*
To the place the streams come from,
*   there they return again.*

It's a rhyme of time by our "glass-half-full" ecclesiastical brother. How can I add to what's already been said except by more examples? The author calls it all "meaningless," and I see his point, but can just as well take the other tack.

What are these cycles but an eternity within time? And they're an infinite resource thereby.

Do we not have what we need, and is there not plenty enough, even for us born so late in time?

We drink the water the ancients did; we breathe their air. From their same soil we dig our potatoes, feed our kine, take our meals.

The cycles of seasons, and of rain, sustains.

Is this tiresome? Sir, try living without it.

What we experience, those who came before us also experienced, connecting us.

Time's a circle, not a line . . . or perhaps better, a spiral.

We each have our turn; we are born, cycling through our stages, and we die. Nothing new about it . . . except the variation on a theme—the distinction of you and me.

Each of us takes our turn on the swing, gently pushed at first, then learning to pump on our own, gleefully striving to fly the highest, maybe jump out the farthest, or just enjoy the movement and the ever-changing scene.

When we get off, the swing set remains, and others take their turn.

We're not quite sure how it happens . . .
why we get to swing at all
or who put the swing set there.
These are mysteries to a child
or would be if they thought about them,
which they don't, not for long,
and neither do we much either.

The mystery remains.

Meaningless?
Maybe.
But through my cycles, I'm changed.
And that, I think, means something . . .
Meaningful.

Whether half empty or half full,
It's still a glass,
and there is water.
Come and drink.

Who was this?
Qohelet?
No photo exists.

We Will Never Fill Up

The eye never has enough of seeing, nor the ear its fill of hearing. —Ecc. 1:8b

We returned from travels and our days were so full after, it's like we were never gone. It's a gift, really, a full life. There's enough to do every day, every hour. We'll never get it all done or get it all in.

At best we come to little levels of "enough for now."

It's a rare day when we climb a mountain that another doesn't come into sight.

Before we even returned from our last trip, we were talking about our next. Pre-dawn, jet-lagged waking from sleep offers opportunity to get something else "done." (Like writing this.)

Every day has its focus. Then there's a plethora of other things to focus on, some left over from the day before, and some new and already demanding mental time.

Besides that, we're passing by things on every side that are so interesting they could involve another lifetime of attention if we had it.

Something I've long said: "I thank God for eternity when I'm running out of time."

In a sense, we're already connected to the infinite; that's why we even think like this. We know that there is always more, more, more . . . and we'll never have it all, see it all, hear it all, think it all.

Our Ecclesiastical sage cited this as just another vanity, but the same thing can be seen as another gift.

Once, deep in rich conversation with a good friend, we got interrupted and had to quit. "We'll finish this later," he said, then added, "we'll never finish!"

I loved that. And though distance has separated us, when we do meet, we pick up right from where we were. We'll never finish.

Friendship, beauty, music, even our "to do" list; these are things that will never be complete. Not completely.

There's always another mountain, but we can only climb one at a time. And the one we're on is likely the one we were hoping to be on when we were on the last one.

So climb it, love it, and take in what you can.

Eternity's coming. Meanwhile, time is gift enough.

A freeway overpass under construction, climbing another mountain.
Foreground, a hoe and wheelbarrow, basic tools still in use.

London Portrait Gallery. Nothing new. Who is gazing at who?

Innovation, Not

There is nothing new under the sun. —Ecc. 1:9

Here's one of the Ecclesiastical truths that's most prominent and most hard to understand or accept.

Could it be that he lived so early that nothing yet had been invented?

But what would that say about the Iron Age, the Bronze Age, the age after age of magnificent architecture and accumulated wisdom created and gathered very early, the likes of which the world has hardly seen since?

Maybe that's the point. The principles have all been laid down from the beginning; the world runs on a certain course, is all governed by certain laws, and nothing will ever be added to them. Anything that follows is only further discovery of what has always been.

That discovery, however, has kept minds busy for generations, with certain spurts at certain times and places. We like to think we're in one now, evidenced by many things, particularly breakthroughs in science and technological innovations.

But the principles have always been.

Take this typography I'm using to communicate with. It's nothing but a bunch of pixels arranged and communicated electronically over airwaves that have always been here. This one was designed by Jonathan Hoefler, but the prototype was first formed by the Greco/Romans and their predecessors, devised from earlier alphabets in various languages.

A lot of this is traceable history, like the approximate date of the first alphabet (around 1500 BC), or prehistory, like the first division of languages from one. But before that? Man's been communicating from the beginning, and there's nothing new about that.

I'm thinking even the term "invent" should probably really be "discover."

For such tinkering, however, I would like to give credit to my friend and son-in-law, Vernon Adams. Vernon designs fonts for a living, and no, they've not all been invented. They keep pouring out of him.

Not new under the sun, of course. Just a new variation on a very old theme.

Face it, We Won't be Remembered

Even those yet to come will not be remembered by those who follow. —Ecc. 1:11

I got an e-mail out of the blue, asking if I was related to one Hyatt Moore who had been married to the inquirer's great-grandmother. She'd been doing some family research and happened upon the connection. A quick Internet search and she found me.

As the number on earth with that name is limited (my grandfather being the first, I'm the third, my grandson the fifth), her research was quickly rewarded. It began an interesting exchange of sparse information and a few old photographs. The late-in-life marriages had been the second for both my grandfather and her great-grandmother and hardly remembered in family history two generations later.

If the inquirer had waited another generation, she would have received no information at all.

There is no remembrance of men of old, and even those who are yet to come will not be remembered by those who follow.

That's how it is.

The memory of me and the memory of you will last about two generations, and that's it. Even then, it'll be only a name and a few facts, and those the mundane ones.

All the good stuff, about what an interesting person I was, and you were, what we thought about, the challenges we overcame, our glorious resume of jobs, the influence, the friends, the books, the travels, our unique tastes, the symbols of various successes and interests and everything else, will all be just the stuff of dust.

My grandfather was a railroad conductor, had seven children, and struggled for a time to make it as a homesteader in the wilds of Wyoming. That's about all I know.

About his father, I know nothing.

Some people can go back farther, and some people make a study of it. But it's pretty normal that before long, it's gone.

Remember *Yertle the Turtle* by Dr. Seuss? Yertle wanted to be king of all he saw so he gathered all the turtles he could—first nine, then 5,607—and got them all stacked up under him so he could see (and be king of) more. Finally, Mack, the turtle at the bottom, broke (actually, burped) and all came tumbling down. There is a point, maybe numerous points, but mine is that in all those turtles, only two are named, Yertle and Mack.

There's me, Yertle—the central figure in my own story—and there's Mack, some ancestor way back there generations ago. All the rest are nameless, and only sort of important for bringing me to my place at the (so far) top.

Sounds a bit egocentric, but don't worry—that'll go too. Soon enough, each of us will be one of the nameless turtles teetering in the middle of somebody else's stack.

No wonder our Ecclesiastes-writing ancestor wrapped it up with, "Meaningless, meaningless."

Except at the end, he said: *Fear God... for He will bring every deed into judgment, large or small... (Ecc. 12:13-14)*

It's a comforting thought that at least we'll be remembered by "Somebody."

I'm trusting He'll overlook a lot.

The mystery of memory:
Somewhere it's permanent,
but not in human minds.

Everything plus Everything Is Zero
—Ecclesiastes 2 in summary

Page one, first sentence: *All is meaningless.* Somebody should have told the writer this is no way to start a book, particularly not one that's supposed to be helpful.

But he couldn't be stopped; he was writing from experience.

He was looking at life from the other side of hope. Not hopes dashed, but rather HOPES FULFILLED!

He was one of those rare among us who was able to achieve everything he could imagine. Most who do that end up disappointed. And he did too, until he saw greater light.

Here's the account in his words, summarized from Ecclesiastes 2:

All
I had everything
so I could do anything
so here's what I did:

Kicks
First, I went after pleasure
and found it . . .
pleasureless.

Laughs
Not enough laughter, I thought,
though it's good for the bones,
it's pretty shallow as a reason to live.

Wine
I became a connoisseur,
loving its pleasure, its nuance, its complexity (and conversation);
but in the end, every bottle is only empty.

Largesse
I became an altruist,
used my resources for the public good,

providing beautiful spaces,
landscapes of lakes, whole arboretums
bearing fruit for the mouth and for the eyes.

Manpower
To do it I amassed a great workforce,
had my own mega-farm to feed them all.
No spread had more acres, more livestock.

Lucre
My investments kept producing.
No Swiss bank account; I had Switzerland.
Nothing I could do could prevent the money
pouring in.

Skirts
Of these, I won't even mention,
Except there were plenty,
always.

Indisputably Top of All
Suffice to say, I had more of everything than
anybody;
there was nothing I needed to refuse myself . . .
so I didn't.

But, though I reveled in it all . . .
making it, building it up . . .
Until I finished.
Then I didn't . . . revel.

The Sum of All plus All is Zero
Because there was nothing else to do,
except write up my will.

And who knows what "whoever would get all

Rose. Just a another sketch and cryptic name.

21

this" would do with it?
He could be a fool and lose it all . . .
and likely so, as he wouldn't have worked for it.

Joy of Work
Then I realized it was the work itself that brought the pleasure,
that, with a little food and drink,
and a certain sense of God.

Curtain Closes
Other than that, death wins,
and what was it all for?

There it is. An opening overview. Chapter 2 of a book with 12.

Whatever we pursue, whether or not we attain, in the end, death wins.

Some have suggested that the oft-repeated phrase "under the sun" explains the whole thing, that Ecclesiastes is how life looks without the light of God shining through. Maybe so. Still, its honesty cannot be refuted.

Here's a take from 20th-century novelist Thomas Wolfe:

"Of all I have ever seen or learned, that book seems to me the noblest, the wisest, and the most powerful expression of man's life upon this earth — and also the highest flower of poetry, eloquence, and truth. I am not given to dogmatic judgments in the matter of literary creation, but if I had to make one I could say that Ecclesiastes is the greatest single piece of writing I have ever known, and the wisdom expressed in it the most lasting and profound."

I could have put this in the intro, but there was no room. Suffice to leave it here, in the summary of all things.

Read on.

Jessica, of Paraguay, and full flowing mane.

Life: The Great Experiment

I wanted to see what was worthwhile for men to do during the few days of their lives. —Ecc. 2:3b

Now there is a responsible approach to life: Consider it as one grand laboratory test.

Not everybody can, or will, but if we have a modicum of wherewithal, live in a free society, trust that we have some years still ahead, and any curiosity about how it would be IF . . . then we can experiment. And should!

We only live once. Much of it is proscribed. But there's a great deal that's just up to us. It seems only right that we take at least a few calculated risks that might eventuate into

something that would never otherwise happen, or be learned. And maybe, daily.

I read a book once on the creative process, suggesting we can create, and even name an "alter ego" for ourselves. That "other person" then has the permission and expectation to try things our own more conservative and more fearful person might never consider. Sounds wild. I thought I'd try it. I kept my last name but took on the new first name of "Risk."

"Risk Moore."

It was to be a reminder that taking risks is part of what I'm supposed to be doing, at least sometimes.

Risk is sometimes another word for faith.

24

The painter Paul Gauguin took a lot of risks. Actually many were irresponsible and in the end he died, singularly unsuccessful and miserable. But artistically, he experimented in ways that opened a whole new way of making art. If he hadn't done it, we wouldn't have it. He himself didn't know what was in him until he began to experiment.

I've let some of what he learned—about strong color and simplified shapes, not to mention the intrigue of peoples in another culture—influence me. It's helped in my own risk taking, which has helped in my growth.

So, I say, experiment. Go beyond current experience.

Keep your moral boundaries intact, of course, lest you be sucked under.

But under God, there's a wide world yet to be explored, a universe actually, starting within our own minds.

It requires a bit of courage, a bit of faith, a bit of imagination. Who knows what will come of it?

Except more life.

Left: Dallas Airport, a guy so engrossed in his laptop he never looked up.
Above: Kenya, Masai women singing, me sketching furiously.

Here's a Gift: Work

My heart took delight in all my work. —Ecc.2:10

Get to work; it's a gift. What? Yes! Our Ecclesiastes author says so at least six times, each as wrap-up of other ponderings. "I don't understand this and I don't understand that," he says, "but one thing I know: To enjoy my work is a gift of God." That's my paraphrase. It's also become my own conclusion.

Think about it. Each of us has a talent, likely a number of talents. To put them to use gives us pleasure, focus, and purpose. Without them, we'd be lumps of nothing. With, we're engines of energy just looking for how to put them to use.

It was a gift from the beginning. Adam was a landscape gardener. And that was before the curse *(Gen. 2:15)*. He may have been in paradise, but God knew he was going to need something to do. The maintenance and rearrangement of the created resources, that's been our part ever since.

A person who has found where and how to make his particular contribution according to his own talent will never "work" another day. If you haven't found it yet, keep looking. Or rethink your current situation.

Work is only onerous when it's against the grain.

Okay, it's always a little against the grain. Very little is "easy." There's always at least a bit of resistance, sometimes

From a clay figurine picked up in Cape Verde, Africa.

a lot. But facing up to the challenge, overcoming the inertia, and expressing our own uniqueness in the process, that's what we do. That's our work, and one of our great reasons for being.

As Ecclesiastes might proclaim: TGIM. "Thank God it's Monday!"

Here are some further quotes from that book:

My heart took delight in all my work (Ecc. 2:10).

A man can do nothing better than to eat and drink and find satisfaction in his work (Ecc. 2:24).

There is nothing better for a man than to be happy and do good while he lives . . . and find satisfaction in all his toil (Ecc. 3:12,13).

It is good and proper for a man to eat and drink, and to find satisfaction in his toilsome labor (Ecc. 5:18).

Nothing is better for a man . . . than to eat and drink and be glad . . . then joy will accompany him in his work (Ecc. 8:15).

Whatever your hand finds to do, do it with all your might (Ecc. 9:10).

That's a lot of restating of the same theme. There must be good reason.

Rest is fine, as are diversions and entertainments; but they'll never give a life meaning.

Even a job that's not particularly wonderful at least provides a rhythm to life, a self-expression in some way, a context for a bit of creativity, for relationship, and participation in some larger cause.

It's a gift. Each of us has something, first to hone, then to contribute. The opportunities are everywhere. The garden still needs tending.

So get your gloves, get your shears, and get going. It'll make you who who you are.

Depending On Folly

I saw that wisdom is better than folly, just as light is better than darkness. —Ecc. 2:13

That's a quote from our ecclesiastical sage to which we might say, "Well, duhhh . . . "

Did it take the wisest man in the world to come up with that?

Light's better than dark. That's pretty black and white. It hardly needs saying.

Then again, there's quite a bit of evidence that we don't all see it that way. In fact, it seems a lot of our society—and economy—is dependent on folly. Maybe we need folly in order to keep certain occupations, and even whole systems, in place.

I've been in areas of the world where night watchmen are kept busy patrolling all neighborhoods. The citizenry divides the population into thirds: one third is hired by a second third to protect itself from the third third.

Sounds crazy, but I suppose it steadies the economy, providing occupation for all.

Without a little folly, what, for example, would newspapers have to talk about?

And what would the courts do?

Or the police?
Or personal bodyguards?
Or the military?
Or the whole penal system?
Or lawmakers?
Parole officers?
Drug dealers?
Late-night revelers?
All manner of counselors?
Psychiatrists?
Ambulance drivers?
Pawnbrokers?
Lawyers?
Pimps?
Pornographers?

Prostitutes?
Arbitrators?
Bailiffs?
Bouncers?
Bill collectors?
Gaming dealers?
Palm readers?
Pergurers?
Slave traders?
Murderers?
Liars?

And let's not forget
about half of the
world's artists and
writers.

Unfortunately, the
list could go on
and on.

Thre's no shortage
of darkness out
there. Doing it,
and confronting it
still preoccupies.
But light is better.

A fellow listener, him taking no notes, me both noting and drawing (as usual).

A Time for Everything

And a season for every action under heaven. —Ecc. 3:1-8

One of the most known passages in Ecclesiastes is the time poem . . . a time for this and a time for that. Then *The Byrds* came along and made it more so, setting it all to arresting harmonies. The truths seem pretty basic really. Then again, there is a certain permission given, not to mention an understanding about how life works. Whatever the situation is now, there will be another later, and likely opposite. Ours is not only to accept it, but to rise to the moment with appropriate response.

The list is complete enough to symbolize just about everything else we could think of. There's a time to be born, a time to die, a time to plant, a time to uproot, a time to mourn and a time to dance. So it goes for seven plus seven couplets. It's double complete. But I could add some of my own, like:

There's a time to sleep, a time to wake.
A time to give, a time to receive.
A time to kiss, a time to not.
A time to be light hearted, a time to get serious.
A time to give advice, a time to listen to advice.
A time to work, a time to rest.
A time for risk, a time to refrain from risking.
A time to be sensual, a time to be coy.
A time to speak up, a time to shut up.
A time to light the fire, a time to let it die.
A time to say Yes, a time to say No . . . and another time to say Maybe, or Later, or I don't know.

But why is this news? Maybe because we can easily get out of balance and think we should be one way all the time . . . like always pious and lose the joy.

There's a time to laugh, but we don't always laugh.
There's a time to cry, but not always to cry.
There's a time for ideas, and a time to put them to work.
There's a time to win, but we don't always win.
There's a time to follow, but sometimes we're to lead.

The person who feels s/he always has to act in a certain way is acting against nature. Playwrights cast their actors that way so we can follow the play, but it's not how God casts us.

30

Life is more full, more complex, with
sometimes calms and sometimes storms.

*Sometimes we fight; sometimes we refrain from
fighting.*
*Sometimes we hoist sails, sometimes we take
them down.*

There's a time for everything, but it's up
to us to know what time it is.

*There's a time to forgive, a time to ask
forgiveness.*
A time to initiate, a time to be passive.
A time to fish, a time to cut bait.

There's a time to pray, a time to act.
A time to spend, a time to save.
A time to train a child, a time to watch him go.
A time to mow, a time to let the grass grow.

*There's a time for everything. And everything
comes just in time.*

Time. We don't understand it much,
but we live in it. We act like we own it.
Rather, it's given as loan to us.

"It's my time," we like to say, "and what I
do with my time is my business." Sounds
impressive.

But whose business is it when your time
comes?

A time for him, a time for her;
and a time for the two of them together.

Beauty, Something we Need

He's made all things beautiful . . . —Ecc. 3:11a

It was Anne's idea, one year, to spend our "anniversary trip" in just one place. Wherever that would be, we would stay there, get to know it better, see it deeper, and just have time to be.

Though it could have been anywhere, we went to coastal Oregon. We were not disappointed. Even with the famous rain, there's also the famous green, the famous

From a Van Gogh, another wonderologist.

forests, the wild seas and wondrous coves, the driftwood beaches, the great seafood and, of course, many interesting people. We stayed three weeks, and the whole time we breathed in beauty to the point we could hardly take in more.

Beauty, it's something we need.

One friend of mine told me how she experienced that. She'd gone to Vietnam with her husband for a military reunion many years after the war. The ravages were still apparent, and after some days she was feeling absolutely depressed by it. She said it was like a sickness of ugliness. Too bad; Vietnam in its natural state is a place of beauty. Finally, she came across one beautiful scene, and her spirit leapt. She revived and was at peace again.

I once met another person who had undertaken a study of beauty. She'd earned an online PhD in aesthetics. Intrigued, I went online to find the school and look at the program. It was there, and the curriculum was both deep and wide, involving a great deal of reading. Far too academic for me. Good for some minds, but I'm afraid I'd bog down and lose the original idea. Instead of my eyes being opened, they'd be glazed over.

I like better the example of a Catholic nun I encountered some years ago who called herself a "wonderologist." Her self-proclaimed purpose in life was to see the wonder of every moment and point it out to whoever was standing near and cared to appreciate it with her.

I wonder if some school offers a degree in wonder. I think I'd like to apply.

Meantime, I can always devise my own:
An independent study named *Wonder*,
with a double emphasis in *Aesthetics* and *Beauty*,
and a course in *Enhanced Vocabulary* to express it.

I know I'd relish the homework.

Strong in Its Kind

Beautiful in its time. —Ecc. 3:11a

One of the areas of multiplied wonder is how everything works, and works together; the ecosystem functions in perfect harmony, the animal kingdom works with the plant and mineral kingdoms, and so on. The science of it all is wonder enough without it being beautiful besides.

But as beauty is pervasive in nature, it seems it's not just an extra. It's intrinsic. And it satisfies something basic in our soul.

God, it says in Genesis, called everything as He finished it, "Good." Such an understatement. We'd have called it incredibly, stupendously, over-the-top awesome and incomprehensibly beautiful in the sublime.

God made everything beautiful in its time.

I take that to mean all things that God has made are beautiful at every stage of time. Not just when they're "done."

I've thought about this in painting. A painting, at least the way I approach it, should have a certain beauty from its first strokes. Then at every stage of its making it could be considered "finished." It's the artist's decision how far s/he wants to take it.

A newborn is beautiful for its amazing completeness as a human being. A toddler, as it develops, is a wonder to watch. Neither of these are "finished," but for their stage, they're complete. It's the same all through life. Each stage is beautiful in its time.

Beauty is in the process as well as the goal.

And what is the goal anyway, but snapshots in time?

A great definition I once read of beauty is "anything strong in its kind."

Strong in its kind!

Beautiful!

Even that definition is strong in its kind.

With that definition we are relieved from having to compare across kinds. Something strong in one category is simply not comparable with something strong in another. The blue-green, semi-transparent ice fields of Greenland are majestic, but we do not compare them with the also spectacular earthen buttes of New Mexico. And we don't compare either one with a beautiful woman. Or a great piece of music. Or a sea anemone in the sun.

I'm told that as Einstein was working his theories, when he was hitting it right, he recognized the beauty in it. Beauty pervades nature, including in the abstract.

We shouldn't be surprised. But we can always take delight.

God has made
in their time
all things
strong in their kind.

I've long thought Tibetans are all strong in their kind.

The eyes blank, the mind turned inward; who knows what she sees?

Imagination—Peep Holes in the Mind

He has set eternity in the hearts of men; yet they cannot fathom what God has done... —*Ecc. 3:11b*

How limited we are in these earthly bodies, with only so much energy, and only so many years. Certainly we are finite beings with boundaries. Yet, in mysterious ways, we are somehow connected to the infinite.

Our brains may be matter, but our minds are more. The gray stuff is sheltered within a shell; the mind, however, is free to wander. And wander it will, if it wants, to anywhere in the world and beyond, or through the skies, winglessly flying.

Imagination:
The largest capacity we have.
How tentatively we venture into it . . .
Our fences staked so close to home.
Yet there really is no end
Of where it can go
Or where we can go by it.

At least that's my thought.

It's another thing that distinguishes us from the animals.

We can't do everything. But we can imagine most anything.

It just takes two words to get things started: "What if?"

Einstein famously said, "Imagination is more important than knowledge." Or was it, "more important than intelligence"? Either way, it all works together. Knowledge is about "what is," imagination about "what could be." Together they're greater than the sum of their parts.

Of all our faculties, imagination is our most expansive.

But for all that, there's more than we'll ever fathom. The "eternity in our hearts" is hint that there's a lot more here than meets the eye, and much more yet to come.

Imagine that.

Envy—More Chasing Wind

And I saw that all labor and all achievement spring from man's envy of his neighbor. —Ecc. 4:4

It's an Ecclesiastical assertion I don't much like.

Is there nothing we do that isn't motivated by envy?

Or, if that's the case, is there a time when envy isn't negative? We have to be doing something! Laziness leads to ruin.

Maybe a touch of competition is just the thing to make the difference between couch potato and furniture designer.

And who, in any field, isn't aware of the champions in that field, living or dead, that set the standards for excellence? Anything wrong with that?

Unless it undermines our tranquility . . . without which life isn't much fun.

Jealous thoughts? Who knows?

And who is my neighbor? The one I'm competing with?

But, I say, I'm not competing, he is! There have been moments when I've recognized that I'm the cause of someone else's jealousy. I don't like that. I want to say, "Lighten up, there's enough to go around." Or, "Okay, it's my time now; it'll be your time after awhile."

But we want it to be our time all the time.

In the human race, can't we all win? Seems there are plenty of prizes, just different categories.

Or is it just more chasing after wind?

The wind always wins!

The Passive Path to Ruin

The fool folds his hands and ruins himself. —Ecc. 4:5

Such a brief statement, nothing more than just a quick remark nestled among the ecclesiastical many. It's such a passive, nonaggressive, "innocent" act—the folding of the hands—for such devastating results.

The book of Proverbs has more to say about this, but I looked instead at other authors. I found much on the topic of idleness and its opposite: LIFE!

Here's one: "Idleness is the enemy of the soul," from soulful Saint Benedict, sixth century.

Closer to our times, but still early language: "Dost thou love life? Then do not squander time, for that is the stuff life is made of." Ben Franklin.

Or by 1800's journalist and abolitionist Gamaliel Bailey: "We live in deeds, not years; in thoughts, not breaths; in feelings, not in figures on the dial; we should count time by heart-throbs. He most lives who thinks most, feels the noblest, acts the best."

I love that . . . deeds not years, thoughts not breaths, feelings not figures in the bank balance (okay, I changed his quote for that).

Note there is no "folding of the hands" in any of this.

"Idleness is the gate of all harms . . . an idle man is like a house that hath no walls; the devils may enter on every side." That's *Canterbury Tales'* author Geoffrey Chaucer.

"Ten thousand harms more than the ills we know, our idleness doth hatch." Shakespeare.

And I love this one, a Turkish proverb: "The devil tempts all men, but the idle man tempts the devil!"

Finally, by 19th-century English dramatist Sir James Matthew Barrie: "The life of every man is a diary in which he means to write one story and writes another; his humblest hour is when he compares the volume as it is with what he hoped to make it."

That's inspiring. And haunting. Excuse me, I've got to run. I have much to do.

And so do you.

In York, England. Every need met. Happily, kitty napped long enough to make the sketch (and long after).

A Handful with Tranquility

Better one than two handfuls with toil and chasing after wind. —Ecc. 4:6

I knew of a lady who gave a million dollars away, saying, "That money never caused us anything but grief."

Maybe she found she could buy back some happiness after all.

Maybe she came across the truth from Ecclesiastes that one handful is better than two, if having two steals the peace of mind.

Maybe she tired of chasing wind.

It's a truth we know deep down, but there's an intrigue that says, "Maybe it wouldn't happen with me," and our mind stays preoccupied with how to fill that second hand.

In time, we learn again that having isn't the ultimate state, unless it's having peace.

It's natural to desire both hands full, but then where's the free hand to do anything else?

And we like to be free.

Too much to keep track of can kill our contentment.

And without contentment there's nothing else that matters.

If, when I go to write my goals, I include "Catch the wind," at least I'll know at the end of the day the source of my ennui.

Peace is life's highest state. We know that's true when we have it; we know it all the more when we don't.

Peace is something within ourselves; if it's not there, nothing outside will supply it.

Not even a second handful!

Family Riches

There was a man all alone . . . —Ecc. 4:8a

We were in England. We've been there many times, but the last several were because family lived there, our daughter Allison and her family.

Whether we went for that or the sake of it being an interesting place to travel is a question. In truth, it was a little of both, but the family part added the richness.

We took a road trip to Scotland. The weather cooperated mostly. We had rain, but with two-year-old Justine in the car, we carried sunshine with us.

She's one of many grandchildren we now have spread around a wide geography.

It's all a growing return on earlier investment. Now to see them, we scrape our pennies together to go and visit our wealth. Or they travel to us.

For the last couple of years we've gathered together for a week in some large house rented for the purpose. That's how we have to do it these days, what with our overflowing abundance.

The deeper appreciation of family is something I noticed in my dad in his latter years. He was always an active man, interested in many things, happy, but not particularly sentimental. Toward the end, it was *family* that provided his main meaning. My father never had wealth, but there was always an even contentment about him.

It's the opposite to the tragic description, emphasized again here:

There was a man all alone; he had neither son nor brother.
There was no end to his toil, yet his eyes were not content with his wealth.

Flying back over the Atlantic, I took in an old classic *The Godfather, Part III*. I couldn't help but note the summary by the rich and aging Michael Corleone, "The only wealth in this world is children."

I realize those without children can still find plenty of meaning. But for me, the longer I live the richer I'm becoming; and the day that I die will be my richest of all.

There's a great contentment there.

For Whom am I Working?

Why am I depriving myself of enjoyment? —Ecc. 4:8b

Here's one for you.

There was a man all alone, wealthy, but without family. He had his work, but it wasn't enough. In the end he asked himself, "Why am I doing all this?"

Have you ever experienced that? I have, like when Anne's been away for a few days. That doesn't happen too often. (Actually, it is too often, just not very often.) At first I'm fine, relishing the time to really focus on whatever I'm doing.

But after a couple of days, I begin to run out of enthusiasm or, rather, out of "reason." Like the writer of Ecclesiastes, I begin to wonder, "Who am I doing all this for?"

It's funny but up until that moment I would not have thought I was doing it for Anne. At least not the projects that have nothing to do with her. But as they weren't for anyone else either, she fulfills (yet another) need I didn't know I had.

A friend of mine experienced the same thing but in a much bigger way. His wife died. After a period of grieving, he threw himself mightily into his work as his whole purpose for living. But in time, he had the same questions: "What am I doing all this for?" and "For whom am I doing it?"

As it happened, he reconnected with an old friend, also recently widowed; they married and are now happily doing things for each other.

Not everybody can do that. But everyone needs someone . . . someone who, if only in the background, they're doing things for. Otherwise, we run out of reasons, and when we run out of reasons, we run out of everything.

Nowadays, whenever I start losing track of what I'm doing and why I am doing it, I think of someone I can dedicate the work to. He or she may never know . . . but it helps me.

Certainly it helps in writing all this, having an idea that someone's out there, reading, reflecting, and maybe finding courage. That's why, in the first line, I dedicated this to you.

Thanks for being there, giving me a reason to be here.

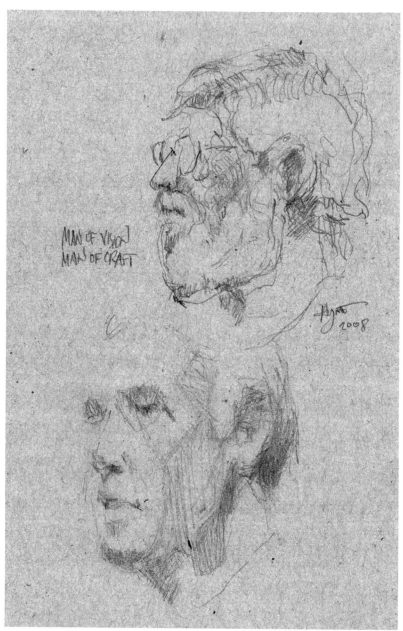

MAN OF VISION
MAN OF CRAFT

My friend Terry Martin, surfboard shaper (top) needed another to get his boards to market . . . who also needed Terry to make them. It always takes two.

Two Required to Make One Succeed

Two are better than one because they have good return for their work. —*Ecc. 4:9*

It takes two people to make one person successful. That's something I first saw clearly while working in Papua New Guinea.

My friend Neil Anderson had stories, and I had a desire to write. We worked together, and a book was born. Not that it was so quick, or so easy, but without the partnership nothing would have happened.

The fact is, it can take a lot more than two to make something complete, but two is minimum.

That doesn't mean that both aren't succeeding. Both can, and will . . . in different parts of the action. One may be dominant and the other supportive. Change the situation and the once supportive may be the dominant.

It's the person working completely alone that dries up.

One artist I learned of tried it. He'd learned he had cancer with limited life expectancy so he gave himself completely to his work. He worked day and night, year after year, completely reclusive, never going out, even having his food delivered. As years went by he didn't die. Except of being alone. Finally, he shot himself.

He left a lot of good work, but to no one.

It was the ultimate non-success.

We all know such stories. And we've all seen how we can't make it alone.

The principle is worked out everywhere. God saw it first: It wasn't good for man to be alone. If nothing else, it requires two for the ongoing of the human race, not to mention the help, the companionship, the conversation, the having someone to do things for.

And there's more. Every response requires stimulus, and stimulus, a response. Every performer needs an audience, every writer needs a reader, every talker needs a listener, every pitcher needs a catcher. Every person needs another.

Listen

Rather than offer the sacrifice of fools . . . —Ecc. 5:1

Guard your steps when you go to the house of God. Go near and listen rather than to offer the sacrifice of fools, who do not know that they do wrong.

There is wisdom in words, the words of another. Often it's best to be quiet and find out what they are.

It's no coincidence that God gave each of us one mouth and two ears. Maybe we're to listen twice as much as we talk.

Fact: The mind is only open when the mouth is shut.

Another fact: Though we can close our mouth, we can't in the same way close our ears. We're meant to listen.

And we'll look smarter doing it. As someone has said, "It's better to be quiet and be thought a fool than to open your mouth and remove all doubt."

The context from Ecclesiastes speaks specifically of our actions in the presence of God, and where isn't that?

It warns of offering "the sacrifice of fools."

What is the sacrifice of fools?

Except maybe excuses, defenses, justifications and blame?

Any of that, when standing in front of the One who sees straight through me, isn't foolishness; it's idiocy. Exactly Who do I think I'm fooling?

If I am going to make a sacrifice, it seems best to start with my ego. It'll hurt just a little, will likely help a lot, and God knows there'll be plenty left.

Best to just be quiet and listen to whatever He might have to say.

Remaining quiet . . . it's a small sacrifice. And a wise one.

Let Your Words be Few

Do not be quick with your mouth, especially before God . . . —Ecc 5:2

Perhaps it's because of the power of words we're cautioned about their plethora. Here's the word on it:

Do not be quick with your mouth, do not be hasty in your heart to utter anything before God. God is in heaven and you are on earth, so let your words be few.

Let your words be few. Not none. We are meant to speak.

But know this: Whatever you think you're saying, you're saying as much about yourself.

Wittingly or not, it's always a self-portrait we're painting. And usually the fewer the strokes, the better the painting.

Speaking on the transparency of every person, Jesus said, "It's from the outflow of the heart that the mouth speaks" *(Luke 6:45)*.

Better to work on the heart than the vocabulary. What's inside will always come out.

Another thing: Under-promise, over-deliver. You'll never disappoint.

Thomas Carlyle said, "If you do not wish a man to do a thing, you had better get him to talk about it; for the more men talk, the more likely they are to do nothing else."

Shakespeare said, "When words are scarce, they're seldom spent in vain."

Let your words be few.

Measure them.

Particularly in the presence of God.

And, as I asked before, where isn't that?

Vows and the Work of My Hands

It is better not to make a vow than to make a vow and not fulfill it. —Ecc. 5:4-6

When you make a vow to God, do not delay in fulfilling it. He has no pleasure in fools; fulfill your vow.

It's one of the few places in the Bible where vows are discussed at all. They don't seem to be so God-required as we might think. Rather, we tend to come up with them on our own, to add power to our resolve. But in the end, they usually only show up our weakness. And when we don't fulfill them, we're worse off.

Better advice might be a shortened version: "When you go to make a vow to God, don't."

It's not that God doesn't hear it; He hears everything. You want to be taken seriously? He'll take you seriously. But when you fail, then what? Here's what follows:

Why should God be angry at what you say and destroy the work of your hands?

Noooooooooo! That's about the most fearsome threat I can think of.

"The work of our hands" sounds like metaphor for EVERYTHING WE DO. To experience frustration with it is, well, frustrating, exasperating, and mega-discouraging. It can make everything seem futile. If anything, the work of my hands needs God's help, not God's opposition.

So what about this?

I've made vows. Not so much anymore, as I know how I am . . . zealous at the beginning, but then, encountering obstacles, my resolve weakens. In time, it's all shot full of holes.

Then I appeal to another aspect of the All-hearing All-seeing: MERCY. And though He takes no pleasure in fools, maybe he'll make exception for just this one, once again.

Jesus' approach was simpler, *Just say Yes or No and mean it; anything else (like a vow) just messes it up (Matt. 5:37).*

So there it is: Just get back to work, don't promise much but deliver more. You'll be on the safe side. Let God, who takes no pleasure in hindering you, bless the work of your hands. It can make all the difference.

Talk Is of Little Use

Much dreaming and many words are meaningless. —*Ecc. 5:7*

It's a funny thing about our internal psyche; if it overhears a lot of our talking about doing something, it figures it's already done.

And causes us to be satisfied with less than what we can be.

I once held a job where ideas were in high esteem. After creative sessions, my white board was so full of exuberant thought, I requisitioned a new one that could preserve the session with a photocopy. My legacy in that job? A fancy white board for the next guy.

I hope I left more than that, but as they say: When all is said in done, there's more said than done.

What we need are examples like Edward Gibbon, writer of the three-volume epic *History of the Decline and Fall of the Roman Empire*. After it was published, people remarked that they didn't even know he had such an interest, not to mention the energy and scope.

The virtue isn't to never voice our plans. There is, in fact, a certain clarifying help in doing so. Rather, it's to be careful about *only* talking and *only* dreaming. The results of such activities dissipate into air. Only action is concrete.

To quote Sophocles: "Heaven never helps the man who will not act."

Or Disraeli: "Action may not always bring happiness, but there is no happiness without action."

Carlyle: "Our grand business is not to see what lies dimly at a distance, but to do what lies clearly at hand."

Emerson: "Every noble activity makes room for itself."

Or from our friend *Anonymous*: "Spare minutes are the gold-dust of time."

It's not what we say but what we do that shows who we are. "Talks a lot" or "Dreams a lot" are not appellations that appeal.

Now, where was I before I started all this talking?

Moderately Awesome

Stand in awe of God. —Ecc. 5:7

"Awe." Now there's a word that's suffered a devolution.

"The universe is ten billion light years across." "Awesome."

"Okay, I'll see you at 5:00." "Awesome."

Can they both be awesome?

Seems it takes a lot to form a new word, but very little to dilute an old one.

("Awesome thought, Hyatt." "Thanks.")

I checked out the etymology of the word and find that "awful" came first. That's "full of awe," basically meaning "knee-shaking fear." But when that word went mostly to the dark side, awesome came along to lift us up. Used correctly, it means "dread mixed with veneration," particularly in reference to the Supreme Being.

Still pretty knee shaking, if we knew.

But it's a result of colloquial weakening that's brought it down to merely "impressive," or "very good."

Or even "pretty good," like . . . "Hey, I got a B on my math test." "Awesome." *

Okay, but then what word do we use when we consider the following?

If the distance between the earth and the sun (92 million miles) was the thickness of a sheet of paper, then the distance between the earth and the nearest star would be a stack of paper 70 feet high. And the distance across the galaxy would be a stack of paper 310 miles high.

Oh.

(Ohsome?)

Hey girl, awesome earring. Sketching (and listening) in church.

Or this:

Our galaxy (the Milky Way) has 500 thousand million stars. Some galaxies are 100 times larger than ours. There are an estimated 200 billion galaxies!

What do you say to that?

"Uhhhhhh . . . "

("Uhhhsome?")

The Ecclesiastes writer, who had a clearer view of the night sky, said, *Your little thoughts and plans are just that; stand in awe of God.*

Just a glimpse of the hand of God helps to put things in perspective.

Awesome?

---

*Actually, for me in high school, getting a B in math really was pretty awesome.

Money, The Unfaithful Lover

Whoever loves money never has enough. —Ecc. 5:10

Here's a truth about one of our favorite preoccupations. But note that it's not really about money, it's about a love affair with it.

God knows we need income, and promises our sustenance one way or another. He also reminds us that a person's worth does not consist of the sum of his possessions. Still, it can take over . . . a one-sided love affair with a partner that is always elusive, generally unfaithful, looking beyond, and just not as interested in us as we are in her.

Looks faithful, but . . .

One defense is to be as casual about her as she is about us.

Anne and I just had another experience with her. We were offered the opportunity of showing and selling our art at a giant home and garden show. Throngs of people would be there, and it not being an art show per se, there would be little competition. Plus, every home needs art, right?

Wrong! At least not in the eyes of those who passed us by with hardly a glance. It's not that we hadn't done our part . . . a full week of preparation, plenty of out of pocket expense, the best examples of our art, all the wisdom we could muster in its display, and prayers. Yet in the three days of the event, we made not a penny.

What's with that?

Maybe it's the economy. Maybe it's our prices? Maybe it's the state of the culture generally. Or maybe it was just the wrong event for us. There may be a hundred reasons, and we endeavor to learn from them all.

On other levels, maybe it's a test of resolve; maybe it's guidance, or maybe it's just another example of the irregularities of life. Nobody's exempt from these things.

One thing it wasn't was a big disappointment. Why? Because it wasn't only about the money. That would have been one measure of success, and a nice one, but there are always others. We made a number of friends, made a few people happy with gifts or encouragements, became wiser through it all, and generally had a good time. When I think about it, my love for those things is a lot more reciprocal than any love affair with money.

Besides that, we never missed a meal, had everything we needed, traveled in a functioning vehicle and returned to a comfortable home. All these things are being provided for somehow.

There are many ways to measure success. Money's one; but not if it's wished for too much. Then the wishing never ends.

The Law of Diminishing Returns

As goods increase, so do those who consume them. —*Ecc. 5:11*

Here's a truth we all experience, whether we've seen it just that way or not. It's a basic concept in economics: The law of diminishing returns.

Take mining, for example. You're walking along and find a piece of gold laying on the ground. Wow. All luck, no work, 100 percent profit!

You figure there's gold in the area and start panning in the stream. Lots of work for lesser result.

You figure there must be a vein underground. Much more work, and maybe now a crew of people.

Pretty soon you're forming a mining company and digging up a mountain. If it's still working for you, great; but the profits keep spreading out to others, and it's a long ways from the early 100 percent.

Okay, you've never found any gold? How about your first car, or your first house? It was all joy, and all arrival. Now, cars and houses later, they're still great, but what with maintenance and expenses and all manner of complications, the joy is not quite as pure.

A dentist friend of mine shared his business with his wife who has a talent for organizational development. While he was doing teeth, she built the place into a full-on clinic. In time, he found himself coming into the office wondering, *What is this, Motor Vehicles? Who are all these people?*

It's just like it says in Ecclesiastes:
As goods increase,
so do those who consume them.
And what benefit are they to the owner
except to feast his eyes on them?

Not that feasting one's eyes on something isn't a reward of sorts. But one sees through that, too, and wonders if something's been lost.

A client of a financial advisor friend of mine told him how he, the client, had reached

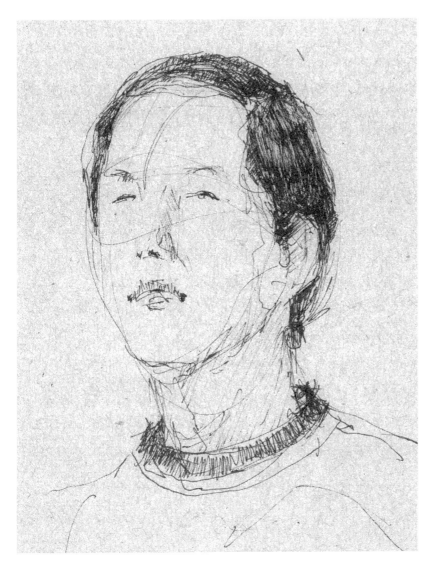

such a state of success,
all he had left to look
forward to was his next
steak dinner.

It's hard to feel sorry
for the guy, but it does
seem like it's the law of
diminishing returns taken
to the extreme.

Here's a Chinese proverb:

*Even though you have
ten thousand fields,
you can eat no more than
one measure of rice a day.
Even though your
dwelling contains a
hundred rooms,
you can use but eight feet
of space a night.*

Best to keep things
simple and enjoy them
100 percent.

An engineer,
pen and ink.

Your To-Do List, It's a Gift

. . . because God keeps you occupied with gladness of heart. —Ecc. 5:20

I once met a man with so much money he didn't have to work. He'd volunteer for things, but when it got difficult, he'd drift away. He didn't have to deal with all that. On the surface it was a perfect existence but, in fact, he wasn't at all content. In a rare moment of honesty he blurted out: "I just wish I had something to DO!"

What a shock! We'd have thought a person with everything could do anything. What this one lacked, however, was the "have to."

Without that, the old ghosts of "What's life all about anyway?" begin to haunt and undermine our sense of worth.

Boredom is a Boogie Man of the soul. It's a barren desert where nothing grows and there's little hope for change.

Thankfully, there are public signs around to remind us to get busy, like: "No Loitering." We should inscribe that one inside our eyelids.

Another useful one we're likely to find on maps at the mall: "You Are Here."

(I always take that as a great reminder.)

As somebody said, "Wherever you are, be there!"

Another classic: "Don't just stand there . . ." (You know the rest.)

Once, when I was young and had the blues (I'd been jilted), my dad recognized it and in his wisdom counseled me to get busy. Just "get busy." Like what? He invited me to Ping-Pong with his friends. It wasn't just Ping-Pong, it was killer Ping-Pong, like when you finish you need a bath . . . in liniment. And it was very effective for beginning to pull me through my doldrums.

All this agrees with a passage in Ecclesiastes about the happy state of man:

He seldom reflects on the days of his life, because God keeps him occupied with gladness of heart.

GOD keeps him occupied. No wonder my To-Do list keeps filling up. No wonder I wake up with ten things to do and by night know I've only finished five, or two (but done ten others not on the list).

This is God keeping me occupied, and calling it a favor!

He knows that too much pondering is too ponderous.

A busy person is a happy person . . . and vice versa.

A ship looks beautiful in a harbor, but ships weren't built for harbors.

We are born to move.

So, get back to whatever you were about to do. And recognize it as a gift.

A stalwart truck, built not just to *be*, but to *do*, just like you.

Having Enough

Better what the eyes see than the roving of the appetite. —Ecc. 6:9

Contentment is a greatly underrated value, until you don't have it.

It sounds so Vanilla when Double Chocolate Whipped Rocky Mountain Mousse is right there . . . just out of reach. Why settle for what you already have when something better is looming in the mirage of your mind?

Well, for one reason, your eyes look better when focused.
Your mouth looks better without the drool.
Your conversation is better in the moment.
And your Attention Deficit Disorder is less obvious.

Question: How much time is misspent wishing things were different?
Answer: All of it.

I read an account of a man in prison who chose solitary confinement so he could better focus. Doing time, he had plenty of it, and didn't want to waste a minute. He became a scholar in his chosen field (Egyptology), communicating with researchers on the outside. He's getting out early for good behavior, well cured of the lifestyle that got him in, and now a man with a future.

Seeing value in the potential of his present situation was the key to everything.

The eyes are beautiful things to reveal what's in front of us. But they also take in a lot of what we don't have and leave us dry. It may be a hodgepodge of mixed metaphor, but the roving appetite is the mother of a sunken rib cage of the mind.

To have "more" is a pretty human preoccupation. But I've often wondered, *Would I be happier? Or wishing for more again?*

Happiness is a present-tense state of mind.

Having all is never enough.

But having enough is all.

A Good Name

Better than fine perfume. —*Ecc. 7:1a*

Jones is a fine name; so is Schmidt. Hitler is not.

It's not the names themselves; they're just words. It's what the person does with it that makes the difference.

A good name is better than fine perfume. It sends a scent ahead and leaves one behind.

A good reputation is a reputation for good. It's earned by many actions and lost by one.

Bill Clinton was a state governor and a two-term US president. But is he remembered for his political achievements or his marital indiscretions? What about OJ Simpson? He had a running good name, for a while.

Reputation is what we earn when everybody's watching. Character is formed when no one is. It's best to have a reputation for character.

Here's an old proverb: "A person with a bad name is already half hanged."

Are there any people with the name Hitler anymore? I think not. Any who had it changed it, or stopped having children. Pretty extreme!

On the other hand, there are names that always carry honor, thanks to lofty predecessors.

I've always been inspired by Joseph, the stepfather of Jesus. Not an "important" man, not rich; he was a regular worker, having a solid conscience and a dependable honesty. He was noticed by few but handed an important role. And that's not to mention Mary and her quiet qualities.

Joe and Mary, fairly plain names, elevated to the heavens.

Our own roles may not be so special, but the requirements are the same: just our duty done with diligence. It's all they did, and all we need to do.

Every name's a fragrance.

Don't stink.

Death, a High Climax

The day of one's death is better than the day of birth. —*Ecc. 7:1-2*

That's a jarring sentence that flies in the face of everything we normally think. The surrounding context elaborates: *A good name is better than fine perfume . . . It is better to go to a house of mourning than to go to a house of feasting, for death is the destiny of every man; the living should take this to heart.*

Consider it: On the the day of our birth we're nothing but a ball of potential. Helpless, crying, wetting and worse. We're a miracle, to be sure, but only a bud of the flower. It's the years to come that will build something unique, a story worth the telling. And we tell it at funerals.

I saw this again when I attended the memorial of a friend. Dave Williams worked with plants and soil and concrete and stone. He helped me with many a landscaping and hardscaping project . . . often on weekends or at the end of the day after other jobs. Quitting time was not a concept he knew much about. His hands were gnarly, his back strong, and his shirt grimy. As often as not he wouldn't charge me, just helping me out.

In appreciation some years ago, I made a painting of him. I called it "Son of Adam," after our first relative, also a landscaper. In the painting, Dave stands in unassuming dignity, holding the basic tool of his trade, a shovel (more than Adam had).

Dave was a basic man. But, as with anybody, there's always more to know.

We learned more at the memorial service where friends and family related aspects of the fuller story—of his early life, his military service, his college education, his prowess as a wrestler, his black belt in judo earned in Japan, his interest in sports (he could name all current players), his love of history, his ever-building vocabulary and his being family champion in the game show *Jeopardy.*

A son of Adam indeed: strong of body, of good mind, unafraid of work, generous in spirit, and walking humbly before his God.

It's ironic, but we learned all this more fully because he died.

None of it existed on the day of his birth.

Friend Dave Williams, attentive in church, not long before he died.

Moreover, all of us were the better ourselves for hearing it.

By odd coincidence, the memorial happened on my birthday. People who knew wished me a happy day. But the real meaning of the day, that which did me the most good, was the celebration of another life . . . the picture of its breadth and depth, aspects of which were acted out in many little circles, each unbeknownst to the other. But all known to God.

A birth is only a life begun. The true graduation is yet to come. When it does, we can hope it helps others, as this one did for us.

Rebuke's Gift

It's better to heed a wise man's rebuke than to listen to the song of fools. —Ecc. 7:5

"Praise shames me, because I secretly crave it." That's by Nobel Laureate Rabindranath Tagore, but I suppose it could be said by any one of us.

And we could add, "Correction shames me, because I inwardly avoid it."

Praise, deserved, is a high thing and should be accepted with humility. For real value, it needs to come from the discerning. Cheap praise is just that.

Either way, it's like perfume; you can smell it, but you'd better not swallow it.

But "rebuke," you'll say, is not just correction, it's correction with a point. It smarts.

And it's smart to accept it.

I checked the etymology. It's from 14th century Anglo-French: to repel or beat back.

We knew all about rebukes when we were children, and we were generally helped. It's a rare thing among adults. We build moats and walls around ourselves that prevent any such from getting through.

But there may be times when a big "STOP IT" would be the best thing for us to hear.

Stop it?

Yes. Stop it. Whatever it is you're doing that's annoying, festering, bringing people down, or bringing yourself down: Stop it.

Sorry if I'm intruding, but I couldn't resist since we're on the topic. I know I need to hear it from time to time.

Take it as from a friend . . . just in case it applies and there's no one around with the blundering forthrightness (or the courage) to say it. If it doesn't apply, save it for another day.

Or, just forget it. I think I hear the singing of a fool. (Much more pleasant.)

Crime's Real Price

Extortion turns a wise person into a fool, and a bribe corrupts the heart. —Ecc. 7:7

As I write this I'm in a courthouse, awaiting possible call as a juror. I have mixed feelings about it all.

Of course, if it was me on trial, I'd want someone as level-headed and pure-hearted as myself. (Then again, I might want someone as merciful as possible, and altogether benign.)

If truth be known, I'd just as soon not be here . . . if nobody minds . . . and let this privilege go to someone else.

Meantime, while I sit here waiting, in another room others are also waiting . . . to hear their cases tried. Who knows for what? Could be for the subject of today's ecclesiastical warning: extortion and bribery.

Extortion: *The crime of obtaining money or some other thing of value by the abuse of one's office or authority.*

Bribery: *Something such as money or favor, offered or given to a person in a position to influence that person's views or conduct.*

Okay, Your Honor, I understand.

And I understand that these things are against the law and do harm

A friend in Canada, before he left for missions overseas.

to other people when abused and taken advantage of.

But that's not the reason Ecclesiastes warns against them. Rather, it's because of their damage against myself, whether or not I'm hauled into court. And, whether I'm the briber or the bribed!

Convicted in court or not, all my level-headed wisdom goes down the drain, as well as any vestige of pure heart.

Here's the irony: The crimes of extortion and bribery are committed because one cares first about oneself. But if one truly cares about oneself, one stays far from even the hint of these things.

Desperately trying to win, he loses. And not just because he eventually winds up in jail, but for what he's become in the process: A self-justifying, mind-writhing, fogged-vision fool.

Not the way we want to live . . . in jail or out.

Meantime, I sit here in this witness-selection area awaiting my own verdict . . . of whether I will be chosen to judge another.

Contemplating sin's true penalty, measuring my own heart.

I plead for mercy.

Another called by the court for jury selection.

64

It Ends Better than it Began

The end of a matter is better than its beginning. —*Ecc. 7:8a*

Here's one that should seem obvious but apparently needs pointing out.

We like beginnings. We have grand openings, congratulate each other, christen things. We celebrate the new year. We commemorate birthdays and anniversaries.

It seems the beginning is the most optimistic moment of anything. In the mind's eye it's as good as completed, and perfectly executed. Being unencumbered by challenges and problems, I suggest celebrating right then . . . it'll never be as pure and unsullied again.

Then comes the middle . . . the months, the years, the eons. That's when reality sets in and nothing happens without work. That's when obstacles loom, doubts roar, vision wanes, fatigue befuddles, enthusiasm falters, early supporters may now oppose, and new ideas seem better.

But a half-finished chair is useless to anyone; so is a house only in drawings, or a journey aborted midway. The list could go on.

It's due to the difficulties in the middle that the abundance of new beginnings wastes away. It's because of this that I always say, "Completing *anything* deserves an applause! Completing it *well* deserves a standing ovation!"

The end is the reason for the beginning. Something new now exists. In the process you've become bigger, maybe happier, certainly wiser. The ends are the reason for the means.

Since this makes so much sense to us, it seems hardly worth the mention in Scripture. Unless there's also a lesson for faith. Like when the day of our death really is better than the day of our birth.

Or that Easter is better than Christmas.

Or that the end of the earth as we know it will somehow be better than Eden ever was.

Take heart. Things may be hard in the middle, but it's for the ends that you've made beginnings.

And all will be better then.

Conflict of Patience and Pride

Patience is better than pride. —*Ecc. 7:8b*

Okay. Sounds true. But what's the connection? We might just as well say, "A bowl of ice cream is better than a bucket of tar." They're not connected.

So what is it about patience and pride that links them together?

Except that they're opposites.

Note:

Pride doesn't see the whole picture but forges ahead anyway. Patience doesn't see the whole picture either, but it knows it doesn't.

Pride considers no weakness, brooks no compromise, sees no obstacle. Patience understands weakness, that it's a human condition.

Pride slows for nothing. Patience does not hurry.

Pride has no patience with patience. Patience has patience even with the proud.

Three listening, don't remember where.

Between them there's a continuous loop, a Mobius strip: Patience fights pride fights patience fights pride and on an on until one of them prevails . . . at least for a while.

Even in movies it's a common plot: The protagonist who is proud is always brought low while the humble, in the end, is raised up.

I've always been glad for those who have shown patience with me.

Including when I've been proud.

Angry? Be Slow on the Draw

Do not be quickly provoked in your spirit, for anger resides in the lap of fools. —Ecc. 7:9

You feel anger coming on? Quick, stand up, walk around . . .
the lap disappears, and maybe the lap of a fool.

I don't know when I've let my anger fly that I've not felt pretty apish after.

Funny, it feels so justified at the time. Almost intoxicating. But as with too much wine, it just looks like a lack of control.

Actually though, habitual anger is a form of control . . . of others. Conscious or not, its threat is used to keep others in line. That's not to say it doesn't work. It wreaks.

Havoc.

Not that there's never a time for it. It is a valid emotion. I like what the Word allows: *Be angry and sin not (Eph. 4:26)*. That provides some leeway and gives a better result.

"The greatest remedy for anger," said Seneca, "is delay."

Anger churns in the stomach by day and at night keeps sleep at bay.

For all this, though, there is an instance when anger is useful . . . when its energy is channeled for good. That's when I say to myself: *I'm fed up with this way of living (what I'm doing, how I'm thinking) and I'm not going to live this way any more!* Such emotional resolve can change the whole life for the better.

But, caution: That's only when directed toward the self, not toward another.

Here's the key—
Keep holstered the anger pistol,
practice how slow you can draw.

Even then, be warned:
You could put a hole in your craw.

67

The Good Old Days (Not)

Do not say, 'Why were the old days better?' For it is not wise to ask such questions. —Ecc. 7:10

Memory, it seems, is selective. It's easy to think the good old days were somehow better. But did we think so when we lived them? Were those days not as full of preoccupation with the future and roller-coastered with the present as now?

For two reasons it's noteworthy that the writer in Ecclesiastes remarked on this: (1) that he saw it, and (2) that he saw it so long ago.

When, exactly, were these words written? If Solomon wrote them, that would be around 900 BC, during the golden age of Hebrew national ascendency . . . a strange time to be considering earlier days as better.

Or, as factors imply, they were written by Qohelet some 400 years later, that would be after Israel's devastation and captivity. Then the early days really were better.

Either way, it's useless to stew on it.

We ourselves could yearn for simpler times, like before power steering, or refrigeration, hot showers, air-conditioning or central heating.

Or politically, like when members of the opposite party were burned at the stake after election . . . and then sentiments (and death penalties) reversed again the next time.

Or the romance of wilderness living that was wonderfully wild, and animal threats were frequent and not just due to a zoo escape.

Or when a chronic headache was dealt with by some doctor boring holes in the skull to let off pressure.

And the dentist used all manner of dull contraption to deal with decay, before Novocaine.

When the average life span was 35 years.

And remember the wonderful plague years.

On the positive side, what about the nostalgic "Salad Days," an expression I've never

A retired North Carolina doctor, looking back, with contentment.

understood, but somehow conjuring things light and green with relish and lovely dressing.

Nice, but just as fleeting.

Note that the writer doesn't say whether the early days were better or not, just that it's futile to consider it.

Why?

BECAUSE WE LIVE IN THE PRESENT!

These are the days of our lives, to make of them what we can.

And in the future it'll be just as futile to look back on these as better.

Have a good day.

Wisdom is What Wisdom Does

Like an inheritance, it benefits; like money, it shelters . . . —Ecc. 7:11-12

When our kids were young, they'd ask, "Dad, what do you want for Christmas?" To which I'd answer, "Wisdom." To which they'd answer, "Daaaaaaaaaaad."

Okay, it wasn't something they could buy at the store, but it is what I wanted . . . that and a few other qualities on that level.

Wisdom is one of those gifts that keeps on giving. If you have that, you have access to pretty much everything else worth having.

Seems it was the source of everything for Solomon. He famously prayed for wisdom as he was starting out, and the Lord was so pleased with the humility (and wisdom) that He gave it to Solomon, and ten times more.

Or was it by his wisdom Solomon learned how to gain ten times more?

Either way, it was the same result.

When our son was young, we suggested that if he prayed consistently for wisdom as a child he'd have it when he grew up.

In Kyoto, Japan, an American speaker glued to his notes. (Easier to draw.)

70

He (wisely) took us up on it, in time adding "courage" and "strength." He got to where, when it was his turn at meals, he would pray with such rapidity it came out as one word: "wisdomcourageandstrength."

I don't know how much that had to do with his later being on the Naval Academy wrestling team, his facing dangers in his submarine and high aircraft naval intelligence work, or his later pursuits for a PhD in electrical engineering at Stanford. But it all seems somehow connected with those threefold childhood prayers.

We're proud of him, of course, but we're just as proud of all of our children so that's not the point. I use it as an example of what wisdom can do for a person.

Here's the Scripture: *Wisdom, like an inheritance, is a good thing and benefits those who see the sun. Wisdom is a shelter as money is a shelter . . . wisdom preserves the life of its possessor.*

The benefit of wisdom is what it does. Like an inheritance, it's a head start in life. Like money, it's a protection against what might befall. A life preserver, it provides basic common sense against that which can shorten life.

There's more to say on the wisdom topic, much more, but I'll save it for another day.

At least, that seems like wisdom to me.

Good Times and Bad

God has made the one as well as the other. —Ecc. 7:14

When things are good, be happy; but when times are bad, consider:
God has made the one as well as the other.

Accept things. Also, accept your emotions.

Be happy, and don't feel bad about it. Smile when things are good. And when they aren't, don't resent the smiles of others.

Easy times and hard, God has made them both.

Note that it doesn't say, "When things go bad, get mad, sad, or like you've been had." Ecclesiastes passed up all those chances for (English) rhymes. Rather, it says, "consider" (and where's the rhyme in that?)

Consider what? For starters, that God made one as well as the other.

Job said, *Man is born to trouble as surely as sparks fly upward (Job 5:7).* It's part of life since the Fall . . . and the spring, summer and winter, too.

Whatever comes, take your bat and swing. Hit, strike or foul, you're still in the game. Or walk. You'll find great grace in a walk.

Happiness, a wonderful emotion. It's good for the bones; it helps the face. Be happy as much as you can and as often as you can.

But when things are hard, accept it, reflect on it, learn, deepen faith. Don't put on a false smile; God doesn't expect it, and it's not honest.

Depth is one of the values He wants . . . and we want.

Good times and bad.
Both are of God.
Try and be happy.
And when you can't, face it, learn from it, and move on.
Either way, things will change.

Irony Happens

I've seen both: a righteous man perishing, and a wicked man living long. —Ecc. 7:15

Here's an irony, from the likes of which Ecclesiastes gets its reputation: *In this meaningless life of mine I have seen both of these: a righteous man perishing in his righteousness, and a wicked man living long in his wickedness.*

I can just picture the old man, having seen so much that's wrong with the world, he just wags his head, eyes down, his long gray beard swishing across his chest. He's seen so much that doesn't compute that it all just seems meaningless.

The fact is, however, it's not over. Every life only sees a segment of the middle of things. In the grand scheme everything is made right, if we could live long enough to see it.

This is irony: Life's rules would predict one thing but then the opposite happens. It's so common that I've sometimes thought life's not just full of irony, LIFE IS IRONY.

Seeing that it's part of life at least provides a sense of detachment . . . and the wry smile that keeps us from going crazy.

One of the things I like about Ecclesiastes is that it observes the world as it is, not how we think it should be. That's true wisdom.

It could also be true cynicism (something Ecclesiastes is often misunderstood as expounding). But a cynical view is not the whole picture either. True wisdom looks beyond even that. And faith, farther still.

Here's another: *Although a wicked man commits a hundred crimes and still lives a long time, I know that it will go better with God-fearing men who are reverent before God (Ecc. 8:12).*

That's faith: When I see one thing but know another. When I accept that the facts are not all in, that the total picture is not yet finished.

So, when I see things that don't make sense, when irony almost seems the rule instead of the exception, I have to know that there's a bigger story . . . that I'm only seeing some section in the middle. My vision may be limited, but my faith need not be.

When irony happens, just smile. The bigger picture is still being painted.

Avoid Extremes

Do not be overrighteous, or for that matter, overwicked. —Ecc. 7:16-18

Here's another gem/conundrum from our writer of ecclesiastical wisdom:

"Do not be overrighteous, neither be overwise—
why destroy yourself?"

What? Isn't being good the best way to be, and wise the wisest? Can one go over the top and make things worse?

Here's more:

Do not be overwicked, and do not be a fool—
why die before your time?

What? Is the Bible implying that a little wickedness is okay, at least if it doesn't threaten early death?

Here's the summary:

It is good to grasp the one and not let go of the other.
The man who fears God will avoid all extremes.

Ah, it's the extremes that are to be avoided . . . on both sides of the equation. Come to think of it, I have seen examples.

Some decades back, I was in an adult Bible class where a guest stated his belief that it's possible for a person to achieve a state of ongoing sinlessness. It was clear he was using himself as a prime example. The teacher, either by dint of different theology or a knowing perception of human nature, took umbrage with it all and said, "Sir, you are sinning right now!"

I don't remember what followed, only that afterward the teacher was removed. Apparently for a lack of diplomacy.

Which one, I ask myself, was overrighteous?

An honest gaze, neither overrighteous nor under.

Here's another, illustrating the other side: A friend once told me how he'd been working on a movie set and had been told not to make waves. In time he discovered that the director was embezzling. He reported it to higher management and he, my friend, was promptly chastised for "making waves."

Strange, but apparently for them a little wickedness was less hassle than too much righteousness.

As for the "overrighteous," I've never known a true perfectionist to be either realistic or happy. One only destroys oneself.

As for "overwicked," it's easy to see how the big wrongs will kill us; but we might as well admit that we all live with little wrongs all the time. (And even they eat away at us until they're mastered.)

In any case, it's moderation that's prescribed, and balance.

You can die from either gluttony or anorexia. The man who fears God will avoid all extremes.

A Critique of Moi?

Do not pay attention to every word people say. —Ecc. 7:21-22

Here's our impurity. We're a spring that pours forth both good water and bad. By nature it shouldn't be. But it is our nature.

That's why the advice: *Do not pay attention to every word people say, or you may hear your servant cursing you—for you know in your heart that many times you yourself have cursed others.*

As Miss Piggy would say, "Moi?"

They would criticize moi . . . with my right behavior, exemplary action, and pure motive? Certainly anybody that would possibly find fault with anything I have ever done or said just hasn't understood me.

Where's their sense of grace, their sensitivity, their larger perspective, their sense of humor?

They should know I'm like Garrison Keillor's Norwegian Bachelor Farmers, "pure, mostly." Or, like Gilbert and Sullivan's captain of the H.M.S. Pinafore, who bad language or abuse he does never use! "Well . . . hardly ever."

So, of course, I'm appalled when I overhear someone saying even the slightest slight against my mostly pure, mostly good show of actions and words. They should at least assume that I meant well, and even did well, from my perspective, which, of course, is the one that is right and true.

Isn't this so with you, too?

People!!!!

Ah, but who can control what others will say? We might as well assume that each of us is part of their conversation, at least at moments, and the grade we're given isn't always "A-plus-plus," even if that's what we deserve.

We know we haven't always judged others so high.

So it's best not to sneak peaks at the report cards or eavesdrop on private conversations. Best to give some space. Maybe we'll receive some in return.

Wisdom is Strength, and Free

Wisdom makes one wise man more powerful than ten rulers in a city. —Ecc. 7:19, 9:16, 9:18

Here I am talking about wisdom again. It's because Ecclesiastes, one of the great wisdom books of all time, brings us back to it often.

Among the things it says are:
Wisdom makes one wise man more powerful than ten rulers in a city.
Wisdom is better than strength.
Wisdom is better than weapons of war.

We get the idea and could even supply others, like:

Wisdom is better than money, because by wisdom money is gained.

(Or saved.)

Wisdom is better than vision because one can imagine more than one can see.

Or, wisdom is better than beauty of face; it continues to grow and doesn't fade.

Wisdom, as I see it, is the sense of what to do and how to do it which will be unique to every situation.

Everybody has wisdom in some measure (okay, not the fool); some have it in spades. Everyone, at moments, can use more, and the good thing is we can have more for the asking *(James 1:5)*.

I ask for wisdom often.

I ask for it when I'm stuck. Often as not the situation I'm stuck in is of my own making. I ask, and it comes.

Wisdom is essential for the creative process. That process starts with a question. Clearly formed, a question describes the problem. Creativity then, is merely a problem solving process, which is wisdom's joyous work.

So, a prayer for creativity has a biblical guarantee. It's a prayer for wisdom. And that

The wise Paul Carden, whom I've often found irresistible to sketch.

prayer has a biblical guarantee.

But back to our scripture: Why is wisdom better than strength? It's because strength may falter, or may not be strong enough, but wisdom will find a way.

Why is it better than weapons of war? History is full of the larger army defeated by the smaller with wisdom on its side.

And why is one man with wisdom more powerful than ten rulers? Because he faces life as it is, not how he wishes it was.

Choose wisdom. Seek it. Sit at its feet.

The measure you have of it is the measure you'll have of a whole lot else. It's free for the asking. Put in your request.

How Things Went South

God made man upright, but men have gone in search of many schemes. —*Ecc. 7:29*

There it is, the best explanation of things as we see them: God started it right; we keep taking other courses.

Newspapers may be having a hard time staying afloat these days, but not for lack of bad news.

I still get one delivered to my driveway. How many times have I muttered to myself, "Okay, I'll give you one more chance to give me some good news"? But it rarely happens.

I've sometimes thought instead of *The Times* or *The Tribune* or *The Sun*, a more accurate masthead would be *The Daily Sin*.

Okay, it's not the newspaper's fault. Communication is the lubricant of a democracy and all that. We need to know what's going on. The occupation is worthy.

I remember a fascination with making newspapers as a child. I'd produce a small sheet complete with clever headlines and brief copy, with maybe a drawing or two. It was before the days of photocopiers, so I charged "five cents a read." I don't remember the news, likely fairly mundane and close to home. All very innocent and "upright."

That was before exposure years later to wayward influences and my personal "search for many schemes." Then my news was not so fit to print . . . not large swaths of it anyway.

Even now, God knows, there's plenty I wouldn't want read by the general public.

That God knows is enough. That He reads it, sometimes uncomfortable enough.

At five cents a read I'd be rich.

But not always comfortably.

Happily there are new beginnings. A personal newspaper keeps coming: *The Morning Mercies (Lam. 3:22-23)*.

I'll keep my subscription up with that one. (Especially since it's been paid.)

There's a beauty that comes from behind the face, a wisdom from within.

The Beauty of Wisdom

Wisdom knows the explanation of things . . . and brightens the face. —Ecc. 8:1

Okay, we sort of knew that one of the definitions of wisdom was that by it we know the explanation of things. But what might not have been so obvious is that wisdom *brightens the face and softens the hard appearance.*

Who'd a thought?

Wisdom is an internal perspective which has a visible effect on the external appearance of the one that has it.

Wow!

Here's an idea: How about a line of anti-aging beauty cosmetics called "Wisdom Works," or "Worry Chasers"? Or how about "Looking-Good-Clear-Eyed-Long-View Lotion."

Trouble is, how would you bottle it, or price it? Economically it would bomb; it's too free.

And where would you apply it, to the eyes?

The wise man has eyes in his head, while the fool walks in the darkness (Ecc. 2:13-14).

Wisdom is a proper interpretation of what you take in, but first you have to take it in . . . clearly. Having wisdom is like having an invisible coal miner's lamp inside the forehead.

Fumbling in the dark can make a fool of anyone.

If I gathered together a list of my life's lower moments (shudder), I expect I'd find a lack of wisdom at the base of them all . . . and a fumbling in the dark.

How does wisdom brighten the face? It looks beyond to the larger picture.

It's the present circumstances that can skew the smile, and projected fears distort the countenance. Wisdom looks farther than both and provides the calm.

It's a "Balm of Calm."

Hey, there's another product name.

There's a Solution for Every Challenge

Don't stress, there is a time and approach for everything, and the wise will find it. —Ecc. 8:5-6

Though a man's misery weighs heavily upon him . . .
there is a proper time and procedure for every matter . . .
and the wise heart will know the proper time and procedure.

Those are three phrases from Ecclesiastes cited in reverse order. It makes sense either way, but this seems the better procedure.

Here's the meaning: Sometimes we've got such challenges that discouragement sets in. We wonder if there even IS an answer. But there is. It's all about a time and order . . . and wisdom will find the way.

When something isn't working, it's basically a wisdom lack. "Wisdom" is a multifaceted word. Here the context defines its use: It's the knowledge of the best time and procedure for any situation.

Timing is everything. The right approach at the wrong time won't work.

Procedure is everything. The right steps in the wrong order won't work.

It's true with simple things and just as true with complex things. The complex ones might take longer . . . or require more wisdom.

There's always an answer. If we haven't got it figured out yet, it's not *its* fault. Don't stress; seek wisdom. It's like with a set of lost keys, there's no choice but to look until they're found! Same with every challenge; don't quit seeking, the answer will be found.

The solution has to come at the right time. When it does, put first things first, last things last, and everything correctly ordered in between.

Not that it's always so easy. If it were, where would be the challenge? Why bother to work, to study, to practice, to get help? These are the things that fill our days, and nights.

The easy things bring small reward, the hard ones large. The really big ones require huge pyramids of time and procedure; but don't lose heart, there is an answer.

It's a promise!

The Wind and Our Years

No man has power over the wind; so no one has power over the day of his death. —Ecc. 8:8

I knew a guy who had two older brothers each of whom died in his sleep without warning. Apparently it was hereditary. Whenever I'd greet my friend with a "How are you?" he'd just say, "Well, I woke up."

We all woke up this morning, but for us it wasn't so big a deal. Maybe it should be.

In England once, I came across some sayings from medieval times, which included, "Sleep is a little death."

Another: "Each day is a god."

Certainly my friend had cause to think this way. I couldn't tell that he did—just working his job, driving his car, playing his guitar.

Taking life too seriously, even when we know the end will eventually come, is just too serious.

For me the term "middle age" gets later all the time, the closer I get to it. Or have I long passed it?

Moses said, *The length of our days is 70 years, or 80 if we have the strength (Ps. 90:10)*. Who knows what his age was when he wrote that? He lived to be 120.

If the 80-year life span was a 24-hour day starting at midnight, for me it's already 9:00 p.m!!! How do I think about that? Pretty much like my friend above (except I haven't even started learning guitar).

There's so much to do. So much to read. I love history. But there's something about all the people in history: They're all dead!

These days, I find myself looking at birth years on the obituary pages. More and more, I see my year.

The World Bank has calculated that in the United States the average longevity creeps up every year and is now 78.2. We in America enjoy the world's highest, but for Bermuda and

If this looks a little like Wyatt Earp, it's because it is, sketched during a play he puts on commemorating his famous ancestor of the same name.

Canada, both slightly higher. I'm thinking that toward midnight I'll move to Bermuda or Canada.

Meantime, the best I can do is eat moderately, worry little, keep love alive, and stay out of the way of fast-moving objects.

It's natural to hold on to life as long as we can. At this writing my mother is 95 and still lives with my father of 97. She moves pretty slow; her eyes are dim, her pains sometimes deep. Still, at moments she keeps up her sense of humor with, "Well, it's better than the alternative."

When they will go, I don't know. Nor, really, when I will. Or you.

The answer, my friend, to quote Bob Dylan (singing Solomonically), is blowing in the wind.

And none has power o'er the wind.

Wickedness and its Iron Grip

As no one is discharged in time of war, so wickedness will not release those who practice it. —Ecc. 8:8b

Okay, this is a metaphor (or is it a simile?):
You're in the army and you'd like to get out,
but there's a war and they won't let you go . . .
so it is when wickedness takes over;
you won't easily break free.

But "wickedness"? Is that word still around? Seems like it's pretty much gone into disuse . . . like the overused theme of quicksand in early Hollywood movies. (Though the comparison works.)

Instead of "wickedness" we'd rather use some euphemism like "the dark side," and relegate the whole concept to non-reality, or to earlier times more naïve than our own.

It's the stuff of stories, like when wickedness so pervaded the earth that heaven had no choice but to wipe it out and start again. Something about a worldwide flood with only a few spared in a large barge with animals.

Or sodomic cities consumed by a hail of brimstone due directly to wild and willful wickedness within.

Stories. Folklore of another world when righteousness mattered and its evil twin was punished. (Righteousness, another anachronistic term.)

It is curious how there is archeological evidence for both of these stories. But no matter; what do they have to do with me?

Except that I am a microcosm of the whole. Principles of nature that held then still hold now. Cause and effect is more than an interesting notion.

Jesus said it: *He who sins is a slave to sin (John 8:34)*. And there's another word we don't much use. Though the concept of slave we understand.

We understand it best when we're subject to it.

Wickedness, a willful act, tentative at first and then, with the sky not falling, continued, exerting my God-given right to do whatever I want, whenever I want. And that's often, even if (or especially since) it's not as fun as it was at first! Because I'm FREE! I'm not drowning (per world deluge); I'm not burned up (per fire and brimstone). Well, I may be a little singed emotionally, or socially, or physically . . . or all three. But, GD it, I'm free to do whatever I want, and WHENEVER IT MAKES ME DO IT!

I'm free, I tell you. Free! Free!! Freeeeeeeeeeee . . . .

(The last word fades away, the quicksand slowly covers over and all is tranquil again.)

Cut!

Quicksand?
Sketched from an
unremembered
source.

The More I Know, the More I Don't

Even if a wise man claims he knows, he cannot really comprehend . . . —Ecc. 8:17

One of the things a wise person knows about himself is that he could be wrong.

I suppose it's a good thing for keeping one humble. A truly wise person generally is humble.

The capacity for my non-knowledge of things is almost limitless. And it's not just me. Look at what our ecclesiastical brother says:

No one can comprehend what goes on under the sun. Despite all his efforts to search it out, man cannot discover its meaning. Even if a wise man claims he knows, he cannot really comprehend it.

The things I'm so sure about that I'd die defending are few. And those, I hold by faith. For anything else I'm likely to vacillate, soften my opinions, see from another perspective, or just say, "I don't know."

It wasn't always that way. I used to know a lot more.

But life kept revealing more of itself. At this rate, by the time I'm ready to go, I'll know almost nothing.

Except where I'm going.

It's an odd kind of consolation, but in the end, it's all that matters.

It's wise to get at least that one right.

Live Dogs and Dead Lions

Anyone among the living has hope. —Ecc. 9:4

It's one of those statements of colorful pithiness that puts everything into perspective. I'm reminded of a saying by an old Irish friend, "Cheer up; you'll soon be dead!"

How could one not be cheered by such bright advice?

And about these metaphors; which do you identify with, the dog or the lion?

The lion here is the king of beasts, much revered, feared by all and fearing none. But the dog implied is not exactly the "best in show." Rather this is the mangy, cowering, rib-showing, scrap-eating beast of shadows that no one owns and everyone kicks. It's a contrast between the king and the cur. There is no comparison . . . except that one's alive and one is not.

Now which would you rather be?

For the dead it's all over; for the living there's still hope. And hope keeps life alive.

You may be in debt, but you're alive; you may come out of it.

You may be working a job you don't love, but you're alive; it may change.

You may be suffering from any number of ills, misfortunes, or runs of bad luck. But you're still alive; there's always hope.

Hope keeps life alive.

And being alive is such a precious thing that even the cur will fight (to the death) to keep it. Too late for that for the lion.

So, even if you've only scraps of bread,
remember the words from that Irish head:
Cheer up [you dog],
you'll soon be dead.

Arf!

Go For It

Whatever your hand finds to do, do it with all your might. —Ecc. 9:7-10

Here's a philosophy of living from one of my favorite quotes:

"Go, eat your food with gladness, and drink your wine with a joyful heart, for it is now that God favors what you do. Always be clothed in white, and always anoint your head with oil. Enjoy life with your wife, whom you love, all the days of this meaningless life that God has given you under the sun—all your meaningless days. For this is your lot in life and in your toilsome labor under the sun. Whatever your hand finds to do, do it with all your might, for in the grave, where you are going, there is neither working nor planning nor knowledge nor wisdom."

There it is, an overflowingly positive passage, right in the middle of life-in-the-pits by the Ecclesiastes Preacher, the dooms-day teacher. I confess I tend to ignore the "life is meaningless" parts. I substitute it with something more like life is hard to understand. I can understand that.

But I really rise to the permission, the admonition, to live every tick of the clock with all I can put into it and all I can get out of it. Especially knowing that clock is running out.

Go, he says. Go with God. *Vaya con Dios.* Go, for God is always going, always moving ahead, never back. He's growth oriented, loving His own invention of time, of which He will never run out, even if we will, and we never know when.

Meantime, enjoy the basic necessities, the eating and drinking. Do them with a smile ready to lift the cheeks of the heart.

Go. Get up. Do something. Consider yourself already favored in the opportunities laying before you. Okay, not everyone can win at every thing, every time, but just being in the game is rather special.

Go. Get up. Get dressed. Dress in a way fitting with who you are—favored. By God. By God! It may not matter much what you put on, what you wear, but why not enjoy it? Dress the part. Even if it's just a *bit* part, come prepared, and play it well.

And your spouse . . . the one you're used to after these years; s/he's still worth your joy, and at moments, the highest joy! Keep love alive. Keep joy alive. All moments matter.

And about work . . . okay, it's obligation. But what else are you going to do with the gift of time that God has given you? Meaningful work is a gift. If it isn't meaningful, make it so; or find something that is.

So, "Go to work," says the Preacher. And whatever that work, put everying you've got into it.

That's it. A simple philosophy, straight out of Scripture, sanctioned by God.

There's more. Much more. But I like this little gem sparkling in the ecclesiastical rough. Ours is to remember it, to run with it. To know that it's all a gift.

Why not enjoy it?

Classical concert in Newport, Oregon. Giving her all with what her hands found to do.

The Race Not to the Swift

Time and chance happen to them all. —*Ecc. 9:11*

Speaking of ironies, here's one often repeated, particularly when we think we were the one that should have won but didn't. Here's the full passage:

The race is not to the swift
or the battle to the strong,
nor does food come to the wise
or wealth to the brilliant
or favor to the learned,
but time and chance happen to them all.

Once, I participated in a "Quick Draw" competition. That's where artists work against the clock to make a painting. We had two hours. Most went off and did a landscape; I, and about a dozen others, chose to do a figure study—a draped model, sitting in the sun. As painting is solitary work, few of us knew how anyone else was doing. When time was up, it was apparent to just about everyone that mine turned out to be the superior work. I was grateful, particularly as I'd not been so confident during the process; but it had come together in the end.

When the judging was announced, one of the other figure painters was awarded third prize. I'd seen the painting. *Pretty poor*, I thought. I began to mentally prepare my acceptance speech. The second prize was awarded to a landscape painter. By then, with just one left, I was really ready to accept my prize. But, to my chagrin, the first prize went to another landscaper.

Refreshments followed. I had humble pie.

I was consoled when many people saw my painting and said, "That one should have won." That, in fact, became my reward. I realized it was better to not have won but to be reputed as the real winner rather than to have won, with a general murmuring that I shouldn't have.

Two years later, I entered the same competition. That time I did not paint the best painting . . . and I did not win. So that approach doesn't work either.

Here's the teaching: We can't control outcomes. While the prize goes usually to the best, there are always more complexities at work. We might call it luck, good and bad. Or as Qohelet calls it, "time and chance."

Time we understand. The right solution at the wrong time is not the right solution. But chance? Where does that come in? We thought it was an ordered universe with predictable outcomes. Without that how would science be science, and mathematics the purest system?

Obviously there's always more than meets the eye.

Survival isn't always to the fittest.

And when we're not always in that category, "time and chance" is another thing we can be grateful for.

Summer Hat, the painting I did for the "Quick Draw."

The Wise Despised

He saved the city by his wisdom, then he was forgotten. —Ecc 9:13-18

There's a picture painted in Ecclesiastes that we never hear preached, but it might be a good illustration for an Easter sermon.

In a small and vulnerable city lived a man who, though wise, was poor and unnoticed. A powerful king came against the city and built a siegeworks to starve the population out. They were as good as dead. Then the previously unknown man offered counsel that changed everything and saved the city.

That's my summary. The original writer wraps it up with: *Wisdom is better than strength.* Certainly it made all the difference here. Strength wasn't strong enough; wisdom was.

He also makes another point: *After it was all done, the poor man was forgotten and his wisdom was no longer heeded.*

It's one of the ironies of life.

How often it is that no credit is given to the one it is due.

Or sometimes it's worse: Rather than credit there's blame. You've heard it said: "No good deed will go unpunished." It's another irony, and we've seen it happen.

It happened at the central moment of history!

Too often the wise are despised. It's the popular who are popular. Wisdom is handy in a pinch. But until then, and after it's, "Let's party."

Sounds sort of depressing if it wasn't so familiar.

It's right there in Ecclesiastes: We tend to forget the One to whom we owe our lives . . . the One that, though poor, was wise, and provided a solution to save.

Let's remember.

And not just at Easter.

Of Butterflies and Termites

One sinner destroys much good. —*Ecc. 9:18b*

Every act by every person at every moment affects change. This is both in the immediate environment and the distant. Scientists and theorists of chaos theory talk of the butterfly effect. According to that, the flutter of a butterfly in Australia affects the weather in Greenland. And so it goes, with everything affecting everything, all the time. The amazing thing is that everything works.

It's even more amazing that it works when some things happen against a positive effect.

Here's the scripture: *One sinner destroys much good.*

We've seen it. More, we've caused it. One person's selfishness empties the bank; an overbearing captain provokes a mutiny; somebody shoots the Archduke of Austria and begins World War I. No small butterfly flutterings, these.

And that's not to mention the more obvious, like the effects of termites and other realities often invisible.

Our physical and environmental sciences attest to the connectivity of all things but won't say much about the moral sphere, that being out of their realm. Our experience and history attest, however, that these different dimensions work in the same way. The difference is that in all but the human realm there is no rebellion, no action independently devised, no going against.

That's untrue in the moral sphere in which we live. Here in the realm of free will and intelligent thought we're faced with moral decisions on a daily and momentary basis. And there's hardly need to remind that too often it's the wrong choice that's made.

When it happens, much good is destroyed.

The miracle is that everything is not destroyed. There seems to be a higher order . . . something we take for granted. We'll call it "grace," not very scientific, and too tame a term for such overarching effect. Somehow, in the midst of the fact that one sinner destroys much good, and there are multiplied millions of such being committed every moment, thus destroying all that much more good, the miracle is that we go on. For the while. It's a grace.

The Fool Fools No One

You can always tell a fool just by the way he walks down the road! —Ecc. 10:3

You can always tell a fool; you just can't tell him much. This piece of wisdom from Ecclesiastes comes with a knowing smile, for who hasn't seen it? What's most amusing is how long ago this was said. Apparently, there truly is nothing new under the sun.

Here's a guy, his robe belted precariously somewhere between his buns and his knees, swashbuckling along in his affected superiority. It's hard to imagine what he was thinking when he got out of bed and dressed himself, at noon, except what a show he'd make. Of course, he's right.

Check the expression: the curl of the lip, the droop of the lids, the mouth in perfect sullenness. How about the shoulders, nicely sloped, along with the spine, and a handshake, if there is one, that feels like spaghetti.

But he's cool.

Not that the male gender has the whole corner on that market. It's pretty common to notice a woman, young or old, who seems to think she's projecting one thing but is actually revealing another . . . the state of her mind.

Funny about our fallenness, we don't see our self-deceptions but everybody else does.

What's inside always comes out, even in the way we walk.

Best to just be sure the mind is straight, then so will be the gait.

Just a guy having lunch at the counter.

Fight or Flight, or Neither

If anger rises against you, do not leave your post; calmness can lay great errors to rest. —Ecc. 10:4

You know how some people get all worked up about some trifle and make you feel like throwing in the towel? Very quickly it becomes flight or fight, and either one can only make things worse.

If we're smart, we'll put weights on our feet, a filter on our lips, and stand there like Michelangelo's David, with stone in hand, stone still, never throwing it.

It's not easy, but the person that can keep his cool while in the direct path of a blow torch may come out the one least burned.

It takes two people for a fight, and if one just won't, the finish bell will sound and neither will be knocked out.

I don't know about you, but I've been on both sides of this equation. All three, really, if you consider the angered, the angered back, or the angered-at that stays calm.

I will say that when I've been angry, justified or not, and strongly acted it out, it's rare that I didn't feel all the worse for it later. Or even earlier . . . if the other person took the quiet approach and chose to be altogether gracious. That tends to change everything.

So, even if the commander is onerous; don't go AWOL. It'll be worse for everybody, and for you most of all.

Be angry and sin not (Eph. 4:26) is advice that will always keep the peace.

Accusations happen, but don't walk off the job.

You'll be the bigger person.

Staying calm in some business meeting.

Kings and Fools Switched

Here's a bad: Fools ascending to high positions and the wise relegated to low ones. —Ecc. 10:5,6

Have we seen this or what? We have our share of problems, but a lot of the world has it a lot worse. And has for a long time.

I picked up a newspaper and came across a story of rising violence in Venezuela, scaring the police. According to the story, murders more than tripled after Hugo Chavez took office, making Venezuela the most violent country in South America. As one commented, Chavez promoted the idea that violence forms part of the class struggle against the rich and the landowners thus it's not so bad. He also considered hiring more police "a right-wing policy," so he wouldn't. (Chavez has died since, but the point remains.)

Of course, it was nothing so noble as "class struggle," more like gang members trafficking drugs and killing police to rise in status and send a message that they control the territory. The death toll for police in Caracas went up 45 percent in a year.

Bringing it home, the police interviewed were family men, with higher goals, only hoping they'd make it to retirement alive. During the story's writing, however, another one didn't.

Okay, there's just one example of how a leader affects the state and well-being of the people. There's more, much more.

An Internet search of the ten worst leaders of state today is revealing, not that they're there, but how little we hear, particularly of the people suffering under them and what anyone can do about it. (By the way, Chavez was not on the list.)

It's easier to consider such power mongers who have gone before, for whom we really have no responsibility. The trend is not hopeful, with the worst of them wreaking havoc in our last century. (Stalin, Hitler, Mao—each responsible for over 20 million deaths.)

But as Ecclesiastes recorded multiple centuries ago, *"There's nothing new under the sun."*

It sounds simple, but another verse says, *Happy are you, O land, who live under a wise king. (Ecc. 10:17).*

So goes the leader, so goes the course of the ship. And peace on board. It matters.

Occupational Hazards

Whoever digs a pit may fall into it. —Ecc. 10:8-9

Whoever digs a pit may fall into it;
whoever breaks through a wall may be bitten by a snake.
Whoever quarries stones may be injured by them;
whoever splits logs may be endangered by them.

These are occupational hazards, and all occupations have them, some more than others. It's a fact of life: There's potential for life-threatening danger lurking at the edges of just about everything. A look at records for employment compensation insurance would likely provide a litany.

But do we avoid doing things just because there's a little danger? Too much caution could keep us all day in our bedroom. (And who knows what could happen there?)

The other extreme is a "devil may care" attitude, one that can bring swift consequences that the devil himself would delight in.

Ecclesiastes isn't warning against the dangers of life, only that life has dangers. And that those dangers are right in the line of what we do.

At least we know the kind they are. He who plays baseball could get hit by a ball, but he won't drown . . . unless he's a swimmer; then he could.

When Crocodile Hunter Steve Irwin was killed by a stingray, it was tragic, but not inconsistent with his occupation. When Houdini survived all manner of death-defying situations in chains and locked cabinets under water, and then died from a punch in the stomach, that was a non sequitur.

But non sequiturs happen too. We just can't be on our guard against them.

Our dangers are consistent with our activities. The wise will be aware of them and take precautions.

But not too much.

One day we'll all die from living.

Use Your Brain, Save Your Brawn

If the ax is dull, more strength is needed, but skill will bring success. —Ecc. 10:10

What can I get from this that isn't already clear? Dull blade, harder work. Duh . . .

Then again, two truths are given here. The first about the tool, the second about how the tool is used. It's the right action of both that will bring success.

Dull tools are a problem, but my bigger problem is the dull mind. I don't doubt there are all manner of things I work harder at rather than smarter.

The word "hone" hits home. Hone the ax, hone the mind; the rest will fall into place.

I paint. There have been moments, not many, when someone will say, "Let me see your hands . . . I want to know what an artist's hands look like." What follows is rather a blank look. Better to ask to see a pianist's hands. For a painter, they can be just arthritic stumps you can tape a brush to, like Renoir did in his later years. When you're learning to paint, it's not the hands you're training, it's the mind. Every time.

And it's so with just about everything else.

Even with the ax . . . it's a very dull mind that won't soon see what the problem really is.

So sharpen, sharpen, sharpen.

"But no," says the ax, "it hurts. You're changing my shape. I like being dull. Get away with that rasping tool."

"No," says the mind. "I like the way I am . . . the way I've always done things. My opinions don't need scrutiny. I like my life being small . . . limited . . . broke . . . (or fill in the blank)."

Any success in any thing implies a certain discipline. A sharpening. A hurtful/helpful grinding.

It's your greatest tool, your mind. Hone it.

It'll give you the edge you need.

Timing is Everything

If a snake bites before it is charmed, there is no profit for the charmer. —Ecc. 10:11

Okay, timing is everything . . . it's a truth we've all learned at one *time* or another. But in Ecclesiastes the illustration used to convey it isn't as "on the surface." What's this about a snake and its charmer?

Snake charming as commonplace sidewalk sideshows aren't commonplace on any sidewalks I walk on. But where they are, I'm sure the performance is as mesmerizing to behold as one would hope the snake is mesmerized too. If not, if the timing is somehow off, BANG!

Or rather, "FANG!"

Talk about occupational hazards. What a way to wreck a day!

As we've seen before in Ecclesiastes, there's a proper procedure and time for everything *(Ecc. 8:6)*. Time itself is one of the great Ecclesiastical themes. There are seasons for everything. There are stages of life. There are times for one response and times for its opposite.

But here timing has to do with the split-second nature of things. So small . . . yet it can be the difference between life and death.

Or even in common parlance.

We know about timing in our everyday discourse, or should. There's a certain protocol, culturally understood, that proscribes what will be effective and what will not. For example, if a salesperson asks for the order before s/he lays the groundwork, there will be no profit for the charmer. Literally.

How about anger vented before one's heard the whole story? Not charming!

Or a joke told during a serious moment? Gauche!

In fact, all humor and any good storytelling depends on timing. And in a speech, the pauses can mean as much as the words.

A charming fellow, though not of snakes.

More: All learning has to do with timing. There's a "readiness" required. And "charming" generally works better than coercion.

But back to our metaphor. Some snakes cannot be charmed, or will not.

Then the timing issue is different, like when to change your tune, or make your exit, or dispatch the threat before it dispatches you.

Always know what time it is.

It makes all the difference.

Words' Progression

The fool multiplies words. —Ecc. 10:12-14

Words from a wise man's mouth are gracious, but a fool is consumed by his own lips.
At the beginning his words are folly; at the end they are wicked madness . . .
and the fool multiplies words.

Here's something to remember: Everything in life is moving in some sort of progression. And the final destination has everything to do with the initial direction.

Thus: Words that start with an early twist will end in a hopeless knot . . . and the fool doesn't know when to quit.

I'm convinced words are the most powerful catalysts for good or evil that we have.

Used wrong, they're also the most dangerous.

The tongue's not just a fire, it's a flamethrower.

Making things worse, it backfires, immolating the shooter.

The words of the wise are cool water, quenching everyone's thirst . . . and fire.

Speaking of words' progression, I'm reminded of a Robert Frost quote:

A poem begins in delight
and ends in wisdom.

And wisdom is its own delight.
(I said that.)

Measure your words, for by them you are measured by everyone else.

Couldn't resist this distinctive profile.

On Seeing the Future—Not

No one knows what is coming. —Ecc. 10:14

I read an account in the news about a dope ring broken up. The lawmen followed the transport lines, including the movement of two truckers ferrying legitimate goods with the ill. One of them was religious, the other superstitious. The latter never trucked until a tea-leaf reader said the time was right. Actually it wasn't tea, more like the exoskeletons of dead bugs . . . something like that. All for a price, of course.

When it all busted up, the trucker squealed, implicating the fortune-teller. They questioned her and she defended with a statement that probably put her out of business: "I only told them what they wanted to hear; I can't see the future!"

There we have it, folks: The true confessions of a fortune teller.

As for the religious one, he should have checked his Book. *No one knows what is coming . . . who can tell him what will happen after him?*

That's another reminder from Ecclesiastes that frees us up (as truth always does). If we can't know the future, and know that we can't, then we can quit stressing about it and get on with things.

It's the present that's a gift. Maybe that's why it's called that.

It's a funny thing about us and God. We who are stuck in the present are all preoccupied about the future; God, who knows the future, is more interested in the present.

Remember, *It's NOW that God favors what we do (Ecc. 9:7).*

The future's coming fast enough.

Open your present.

It's a gift.

Leaders and Followers

Blessed are you, O land whose king is of noble birth. —Ecc. 10:16-17

Woe to you, O land whose king was a servant
and whose princes feast in the morning.
Blessed are you, O land whose king is of noble birth
and whose princes eat at a proper time—
for strength and not for drunkenness.

Interesting comment. Could summarize it with, "As go the leaders, so go their followers, and so affected is everybody else."

And who isn't a leader in some capacity? And a follower in another.

A leader has some privilege, that's a given; but better is the one who remembers why he's there. Take the term "prime minister." Doesn't "to minister" mean "to serve"? Doesn't "prime minister' mean "prime servant"?

I read a book entitled *Madmen of History*,* a devastating account of some of the world's notorious despots, every one of whom left their country in shambles, and sometimes large swaths of the world. The book delves into the person's upbringing and family history. None came from a healthy family. And none knew anything about servanthood.

The whole "noble birth" notion versus "servant born" is something we might want to take issue with. Aren't there examples in history where the low born rise to a very high place and deserve praise for both their ability and deportment? Yes, and we love them all the more because they are exceptions.

But the servant in the quote above, though now in power, is continually compensating, always needing validation, abusing privilege, flaunting, and forever lording over.

We've seen this. We may have suffered under it. Or, are.

On the other hand, the leader with an unassuming, natural confidence comes with little need to prove himself . . . and his followers will have much to thank for it.

So, to reword the quote:

All sympathy to you, O citizen, employee, child, (or fill in blank) whose king, boss, parent, (or fill in blank) behaves in ways that are self-defeating and irresponsible to the point of your bewilderment and the hampering your your growth and freedom.

At least recognize it for what it is . . . and do be careful that your own approach to leadership does not carry on the same curse.

Are you a leader?
It's a role most needed.
You're already on top, so put yourself under.

Be a prime minister indeed.

———————————

*Author, Donald D. Hook

Sketched in some meeting: Leader or follower, I don't remember..

As the sketch-book notes, this is not my friend's old neighborhood! But it's all well kept, given the environment.

SHIPIBO
SAN FRANCISCO, PERU
THANKSGIVING DAY

Confronting the Second Law

If a man is lazy, the rafters sag; if his hands are idle, the house leaks. —Ecc. 10:18

Some years ago, I had occasion to return to a neighborhood of a childhood friend. The houses were a generation older now and a bit run down. The grounds were unkempt and there was all manner of clutter. I figured it was just the way it goes . . . it's the second law of thermodynamics.

You'll remember the first law, the one that states that nothing new is being created. (I don't hear that one quoted so much these days, and the word "created" is a political no-no in certain circles.)

But the second law, who could refute? As it states, all matter deteriorates, all energy runs down; things rust, die, go back to dust. It's an easily observable fact of life.

As I continued on down the street, I came across one house that stood out for its cleanness. It had good paint, a manicured yard and no clutter. It was the epitome of neatness, and all the more distinctive for the setting it was in. What it spoke of was the people who lived inside.

I never saw them, or anybody else that day. But the difference between these neighbors was obvious. All the houses were old, all being built at the same time. For most, the second law was taking over, but the one that stood out as the exception proved it didn't have to be that way.

What was the difference? A decision to do something. A low tolerance for clutter. Somebody's better self-esteem. In the end, it was energy . . . human energy . . . confronting the downward cycle and taking time for and expenditure on maintenance and renewal. Three cheers for the maintenance man!

I've not just been in neighborhoods, but whole countries, where the maintenance man is not esteemed. Or he isn't there. Or he's sleeping late. Or waiting for someone else. Like the government. Or whatever.

In truth, what with the overwhelming forces of that second thermodynamic law, it's heartening that we have any influence on it at all. But we do.

That is, if we can overcome that same law within ourselves.

Money, the Answer to Everything?

A feast is made for laughter, and wine makes life merry, but . . . —Ecc. 10:19

I once won a bet of a lobster dinner that there was a verse in the Bible that said, "Money is the answer to everything." It just seems so out of place, more like the title of a self-help book for the would-be-rich. My friend took me up on the bet . . . and later treated me to a lobster dinner!

The verse is in Ecclesiastes (of course) and I must confess I was just as surprised as my lobster-cooking friend when I first came across it.

But isn't the Bible the book that says, "Money is the root of all evil"?

Look again. The full quote is, "The *love* of money is the root of all evil" *(1 Tim. 6:10).*

Money itself is just a fact of life, something necessary for living, and almost always the solution when a lack of it is the problem.

Here's the text:

A feast is made for laughter,
and wine makes life merry,
but money is the answer for everything.

Everything has a use. The purpose of a feast is to lighten the heart. The purpose of wine, similar. But the purpose of money is to make it all happen . . . to rent the space, send the invitations, buy the food and wine, provide the service, the candles, the music, the decorations, pay the staff, tip the help, dress for the occasion, and attend to all the other details for which, if there is no money, there is no feast.

You knew all along that money was a very important part of life; you just didn't know it was in the Bible.

It was in early adulthood I formed a simple philosophy about money and its preoccupation. I said:
"I hate to worry about money;
and the best way not to worry about money . . .
is to have enough!"

Somewhere in Bermuda, with money enough for the bus.

Of course, "enough" can be a sliding scale and be ever elusive, but that's a problem of a different nature.

Enough is what you need; and when you don't have it you need to do something about it. That's where wisdom comes in, and work, and a combination of many things, all starting with a decision.

But with enough, you need not always strive, and need not ever worry.

It's the one who has too little money who is perennially preoccupied with it. Having enough is an answer for that too.

And an occasional lobster dinner.

Little Birds and Whispered Words

Do not revile the king even in your thoughts. —Ecc. 10:20

Do not revile the king even in your thoughts,
or curse the rich in your bedroom,
because a bird of the air may carry your words,
and a bird on the wing may report what you say.

Where'd that bird come from? And where did it go?
I didn't even notice it was here. Just a bird.

That's what the German Nazis should have been saying to themselves if they wanted to keep their secrets secret, stationed as they were in the frozen north of Norway. As it happened, WWII Germans used a system of anti-submarine nets to protect their bases from submarine attacks. The Allies knew these nets existed but needed to know exact details on their location and at what depth they were. So . . . local *Sami* people were used to 'map' these fjord defenses for the Norwegian resistance, who then passed on the info to the Allies.

The point was that to the Germans, these Sami were simple subhumans in crude canoes, trying to catch fish. The Nazi racial paradigm didn't enable them to see anything serious in the primitive culture and practices of these people. In reality, the Sami were plumbing the fjords they already knew so well, measuring depths and taking detailed notes in their head and by making notches on sticks, etc.

It's funny to think of it, but the Nazis should have been reading Ecclesiastes 10:20. So should we.

We should know that there's nothing hidden that won't be revealed. We should know that we actually control very little. And we should know that attempts at damage control after the fact only make us look worse.

What's inside always comes out . . . even our private thoughts. It's best to do what Jesus recommended: Clean up the inside of the cup, then there's no need to worry about how the outside looks.

And we won't have to worry about those little birds
carrying our words
where we'd rather they not be heard.

Cast Your Bread on the Waters

After many days you will find it again. —Ecc. 11:1

I've learned a lot about life from fishing. One is, "When chumming, be extravagant."

Chumming is the strategy of throwing bucketfuls of very small fish over the side of an oceangoing fishing boat to attract big fish. If the fishermen don't do it, chances are slim that any fish will come their way.

So often, if not always, illustrations from the natural world also fit the spiritual. And here it is in Ecclesiastes: *Cast your bread on the waters, for after many days you will find it again.*

Why "bread," I don't know, unless it was bread that was lacking. That's how it works.

One time, many years ago, in the midst of a particularly challenging time financially, I was moved in my spirit to give away my boat. "What? My sailboat?" It was a beautiful mahogany-hulled racing sloop that I'd long loved. But we were going through a life change and moving to a place where it wouldn't be useful; and when I asked what to do with it, this is what I heard in my mind, "Give it away." So after a moment's wrestling, and checking with Anne, I committed to go through with it. We donated it to a worthy cause, which sold it and used the money.

We were no poorer for doing it, and possibly a good deal richer in the soul. It was years later that it began to dawn on me that every time I came near water, whether lake, river or ocean, a boat was provided for our pleasure, and for however long we wanted to use it.

I could wonder if the translation should have been, "Cast your *boat* upon the waters and after many days . . ." except I've seen this reality happen in many, many ways, both tangible and intangible. It's got to be the best of all investment strategies.

Funny how it can be so scary at the front end. All it is is a risk! All it requires is faith!

(That's real faith . . . the action kind.)

"But what if I get it wrong?" I ask. "What if my motive is selfish?

Seems to me we'll never get those motives completely pure. A certain self-interest is built into every one of us . . . and built into the promise. "But what if it doesn't work? What if after all the chumming, I get no big fish, and all the little fish are gone too!"

Yes, doubt undermines. If doubt wins, there will be no chumming at all. And no big fish.

Giving costs. Spreading the bread involves faith. We're dealing here in the invisible world where our physical eyes don't serve. In fact, they work against us.

Who can say what's really going on in the invisible world? Except this: "Not nothing." Behind the scenes the tiniest detail matters, nothing goes unnoticed, and after many days, every investment receives return.

You can bank on it.

Spread your bread.

South America, waiting..

Things Are What They Are

Whether a tree falls to the south or the north, in the place where it falls, there it will lie. —Ecc. 11:3

Things happen. Why they happen one way and not the other is beyond anyone's control. Sometimes they're inconvenient, sometimes disastrous. Either way, they just are.

How much in life do we really control?

Our attitude, maybe, or our response to things, and that's hard enough.

It may be the thing you're chaffing at right now is in the category of things that can't be changed.

We can only change our mind.

The kinds of things beyond our control include:
The weather
Taxes
Other people
That building blocking our view
The reality that "right or wrong, he's still the boss"
That life includes pain
Taxes
Our past
Aging
Barking dogs
The speed limit
Taxes
Death
Taxes

These are just a sample of the things that are what they are. To recognize what we can't change is a step toward acceptance. And acceptance is grace.

We should all want to grow in grace.

We should also note the kind of things that just are but we're well used to, like the race we were born into and the times, our country of origin, our gender. We had no choice in a great many things; we just accept them and go on from there.

Here are more from Ecclesiastes:

Who can straighten what is crooked? (7:3).

What is twisted cannot be straightened (1:15).

Whoever watches the wind will not plant; whoever looks at the clouds will not reap (11:4).

Accept these things.

But don't sit idle. Identifying what can't be changed may just be context for action.

Things are what they are, but still there's work to be done, life to be lived.

We recognize the things we can't change, accept them, and go from there.

It's just another thing that is.

The color of our skin . . . it is what it is.

The Unfathomable and the Freezer

You cannot understand the work of God. —Ecc.11:5

As you do not know the path of the wind,
or how the body is formed in a mother's womb,
so you cannot understand the work of God,
the Maker of all things.

As I write this Anne is in the kitchen cleaning out the freezer. Me, I'm doing the lofty things—contemplating God and the universe.

I've often been intrigued with the passage above. It's right out of the Bible, the book that talks the most about knowing God. The point isn't that we can't know God, the Bible is all about knowing God; it's just that there's infinitely more to know.

Any person or generation not ready to admit this is shortsighted at best, and arrogant at worst. Or maybe it's just "human."

"God," says an old hymn, "hides Himself in light."

No wonder we can't see Him. Or do we . . . in everything? And what about the universe beyond . . . where we can barely see . . . or not at all?

Is God way out there and way in here too? Is He keeping the cosmos together and at the same time aware of (and concerned with) my little plans and worries?

If the wonders of nature weren't enough to bowl us over, what about the not-just-imaginative speculations into parallel universes, quantum physics, chaos theory, and mathematically dividing infinity by infinity?

It's finding real evidences of such phenomena that certain very bright minds among us are grappling with. And what about the mind itself? It's a deep mystery . . . not to mention the brain that carries it . . . an inner galaxy in gray mud that no one understands.

I recall the words of some mystic: "Lord, who are you? And for that matter, who am I?"

It's all beyond knowing.

For now, I think I'll go help Anne clean the freezer.

Try Things—You Never Know

You do not know which will succeed. —Ecc. 11:6

Here's another bit of clear wisdom that, once discovered, became for me a basic approach for how to live life. That's in spite of not always knowing the clear way forward (which is a lot of the time).

Sow your seed in the morning, and at evening let your hands not be idle,
for you do not know which will succeed,
whether this or that, or whether both will do equally well.

There it is, from the highest authority. We're advised, even exhorted, to get into action even though all we have is blind faith and an idea, or the problem of too many options.

There are no promises in this life for 100 percent success every time. That's what we'd like. Somehow we think God should give it to us. Particularly if we're friends. But that's not how this scripture says it works.

Rather it says, "Try things. Try multiple things." If they all work, get ready for time management.

There are no guarantees, except this: If you do nothing, nothing will happen.

Somehow knowing that life is a big experiment is liberating, even exhilarating. I don't have to wait until everything is perfectly lined up, until all the questions are answered, and when I'm good enough, smart enough, rich enough, confident enough. If I'm always waiting for all that, it could be all week before I do something, or all year.

Or all of life.

God created human beings, not automatons. And here He's calling us to remember that.

We've been given brains, emotions, and wills. We're not just subject to instincts. That's for the animals. They just do it. No decision. (Or indecision.) We, however, live in a less sure landscape. Ours is to use the head, explore the options, and then move out . . . in one direction or the other.

Or both in their time.

We can't know how it will go;
and that's somehow a comforting
thing to know.

We've been given permission—
even admonition—to experiment,
to explore, to initiate, to delve.

If we try enough things,
something's bound to work. Even
stumbling along is progress.

Without the sails set, the rudder
is useless.

So, what is it that's been in your
mind to do but you haven't for
one reason or ten? That's a seed.
It's the Author of Life that's
telling us to get that seed in the
ground . . . in the morning. Then
get another in the ground in the
evening. You don't know which
will take. In time, you could have
a garden, or an orchard.

Or the whole "North 40."

A little dipping
the feet in the
water, just to try
things.

Light Is Sweet

It pleases the eyes to see the sun. —Ecc. 11:7

When Claude Monet painted his series of haystacks, he wasn't looking at the hay, he was looking at the light.

What more mundane subject could he have chosen? A haystack. No one leaning against it, as in a Van Gogh or a Millet. Just a haystack. He did 25 of them. All are luscious and each different, because of the different time of day and season he chose to paint them in.

Monet saw the light.

He saw how changes in light changes reality, at least our sense of it. He learned to paint fast. In plein air painting, *reality* keeps changing. Shadows shift from one side to the other. Depending on cloud cover or the sun's angle, different colors come out or recede. He would finish a painting in an hour and a half, or continue it the following day at the same spot and the same time.

Light is essential for painting. Even more, light is essential for living.

It's not for nothing our eyes are called "organs of light." Without their counterpart in nature, they'd be nothing but little dust catchers, annoying soft spots in hard heads.

Eyes and light dance together. Without light, there's only night. With it, everything is ours.

In all creation, light was first, and the way opened for the rest.

Because of it, every morning's a new birth; for its waning, every evening a little death.

The ancient writer never considered whether light was particle or wave (nor are we very sure) but he did know this:

Light is sweet, and it pleases the eyes to see the sun.

He who sees it is enlightened. And enriched.

It's another gift that's free.

Enjoy your Years

However many years a man may live, let him enjoy them all. —Ecc. 11:8

I've been realizing for some time that I'm in what I can only describe as a level state of contentment and happiness.

In many ways it's been so all along; I've been happy mostly, and content.

Once, some years back, I told a friend, "I have everything I want . . . except the fulfillment of my goals."

That seemed to be about as good as it gets, since a person needs to have goals, and a goal isn't a goal if it's already been met.

What I'm beginning to realize now, however, is the "level state," a relaxation on even the goals.

Is this natural? Is it something that comes from being a certain age?

I'm long past any midlife crisis. I had one once.

It was the day before I would turn 39. That meant I'd be 40 in just a year. Forty seemed like the classic age by which something major should be accomplished. I knew one year is not long enough to accomplish anything significant. I sensed panic, and despair. I experienced deeply what I'd heard others around this age experience, sometimes for a very long period, sometimes manifesting in very erratic actions. It was no laughing matter.

By the end of the day, however, I began to regain equilibrium. I reminded myself that in fact I had done a few things, things big enough to have satisfied at least midlevel goals, and that time was not "up"; there would be years enough to get a few more things in. With that, I relaxed. My midlife crisis, intense as it was, had lasted just one day!

That was a long time ago. I suppose I could recount what I've been able to experience since which I or somebody might call "significant." But, in fact, that exercise doesn't interest me much. We live in the present.

The difference between then and now, as I started out to say, is that now I'm not sensing

On a road trip through Wales

any particular unmet goals. And I'm satisfied with that.

We have plans, to be sure, but generally not more than a few months out, or weeks. Every day, I wake with a sense of focus for that day. There's rarely—actually never—any down time. The hours are all full, and pretty much with what I want to do. It's a gift of God.

Is this maturing of life beyond goals also a gift of God?

Don't misinterpret; I know there are areas of my life that could go a lot further. Areas of generativity, of perspective, of patience, and all the spiritual areas. And I'm interested in their pursuit. But these are not goals, per se, as they will never be met.

Today I flipped open to a page of a book I've only flipped through before. On the cover is a label describing it as "The Number One Business Book of the Year!" The page I came to was about "the purpose of a business," where the author says the purpose of owning a business is quite different from the purpose of the business itself. The purpose of a business is basically to acquire customers, to retain customers, and make a profit. But the reason for wanting to own a business, he says, is to create a lifestyle for oneself.*

And that's when I saw clearly that the lifestyle I would create for myself is the one I'm living. That is, the list of things that I want and the list of things I have are the same list.

It's a gift of God, an obedience to Scripture, and a nice thing to realize.

---

*Making Money is Killing Your Business, by Chuck Blakeman

Wild Oats and the Harvest

Follow the ways of your heart and whatever your eyes see, but . . . —Ecc. 11:9-10

Be happy, young man, while you are young,
and let your heart give you joy in the days of your youth.
Follow the ways of your heart and whatever your eyes see,
but know that for all these things God will bring you to judgment.

I can just picture this scene, a gray haired old gentleman at a table on a sidewalk café, acknowledging the carefree youth at the next table who is smoking his cigarette, drinking whatever, and espousing his happy life of "devil may care." I can picture it because it's clear memory.

The old man, a retired architect of old world sensibilities was a man I respected, and there was enough respect in return that he deigned to address some of my foibles. I tossed them off, of course.

He didn't, but he could have espoused the whole passage quoted above: "Go ahead, do whatever you want . . . but know there are consequences."

"But." There's that word, always messing up the freedom, negating the compliment, bringing things back to reality.

And so it is here in the ecclesiastical quote, a permission to live epicurean . . . with a careless zest like there's no tomorrow.

But, it reminds, there is a tomorrow.

Thanks to a number of obstacles and pains, not to mention an invisible "guiding hand," I got off that track and onto another destined to a better place.

It was not so, apparently, with my friend Steve.

I met Steve in 7th grade. He was my first bad influence. He was so clever, so impishly devious, I couldn't help liking him. He needed better influences and I thought for a while I could provide that. But (there's that word again), it went the other way.

We spent years together as friends before drifting apart, both of us getting all the more creative and going on to worse. Fortunately, as I said, I changed tracks. Unfortunately, apparently he never did.

It was years later, like maybe 40, then serving as president of a large mission organization, I was asked to speak at a church some distance away. To the surprise of both of us, I ran into the sister of my old friend Steve. She was church secretary. I asked about her brother.

"We see him from time to time," she said. "He lives in the next town, under a tree."

"Under a tree?"

"Yes, he comes by sometimes, sometimes with one woman or another, usually needing money. He can be pleasant enough when he's not strung out on something, but that's not often."

I never saw Steve, my visit was brief, but I've often reflected on his life, the road he was on and never got off of, and the destination it took him to.

He had fun when he was young, but he never saw, or listened to, the big 'but' in the equation.

Every road leads somewhere. In the end, everything matters.

A young man across a room, contemplating his harvest?

Symbolic Speech for You Know What

Remember your Creator before the pitcher breaks, the bucket's kicked, and all the rest. —Ecc. 12:1-7

There's a passage on the last page of Ecclesiastes that reminds us to remember the One most important to remember while we've still got something to remember with.

Got that?

The author uses all manner of symbolic speech, some of which we can understand, the rest just by gist.

(Of course, we never use symbolic speech.)

Remember your Creator in the days of your youth, before the days of trouble come and the years approach when you will say, "I find no pleasure in them."

Okay, that's clear enough, and fair warning. I've seen where long life doesn't seem so much a gift when pleasures are gone, along with energy, interests, and everything else.

He continues:

Before the light of the sun and moon and stars grow dark, (symbolic for not waiting until you're blind before you start looking),

and the clouds return after the rain, (as when one season of dreariness is followed by another, and setbacks follow setbacks),

when the grinders cease because they are few, (like when food holds little interest and there's little to chew with if it did),

and when the doors to the street are closed and windows blurry, (with eyesight failing, not being able to get out and nothing's worth getting out for anyway),

when men rise up at the sound of birds, but all their songs grow faint, (it's the middle of the night and sleep won't return, and the ears get harder of hearing),

when men are afraid of heights and of dangers in the streets, (when your stooping height is barely five feet, the hip can break and down you go, and every step's a hazard), *when the almond tree of your head blossoms,* (the hair turning white and falling out),

when the grasshopper drags himself along, and desire is no longer stirred, (can't imagine what that is symbolic for . . . or at least don't want to contemplate it).

Sketched in Anchorage, Alaska.

It's all rich with symbolism, offered to get us to take most seriously the most serious thing we can . . . before the jig is up, the bucket's kicked, the dust is bit, the chips are cashed, the farm is bought, the Grim Reaper met, the ghost given up, we've breathed our last, taken our bow, we're six feet under, we're pushing up daises, and our bodies are fodder for worms.

Did I say we don't use symbolic speech?

Okay, let's get concrete: To date, 99,000,000,000 people have died.

The mortality rate is still 100 percent.

Remember your Creator in the days of your youth.

Your graduation date is scheduled.

Do your homework.

Words: Goads and Nails

They're tools of the wise . . . to motivate, to build, to seal, to breathe life or kill. —Ecc. 12:11

The words of the wise are like goads, they're collected sayings like firmly embedded nails —
given by one shepherd.

Now there's a mix of metaphor. And simile. The similes I understand: Wise words are *like* goads, driving us on; they're *like* nails, pounded in and fastened.

But by a shepherd?

Apparently this is one multi-talented sheepherder, and multi-tooled.

And the sheep? I guess that's dull-witted us.

But my thoughts today are about the words themselves. Whether we're a shepherd or a sheep, words are extensions of ourselves, and the most powerful tools we have. With them, we both create and destroy.

Seems they're the most powerful things God has too. He said, "Let there be . . ." and all came into being.

In a similar way, we do the same. At the beginning of anything, we voice our ideas. It may be only to ourselves, but after that a new thing is born.

By her words she creates, or destroys.

125

They also destroy. "Off with her head!" said the Queen of Hearts, too glibly and too often. We, I'm afraid, are guilty of the same. It's by our words that we murder and maim.

Words are strong, even when soft. We use them casually, absently, too often foolishly. The wise use them with care, and often not at all.

Words are goads and nails, and a whole lot more.

Goads of the guide, leading from behind
Nails of the parent, driving lessons home
Fertile field of the poet
Molding clay of the teacher
Scepter of the leader
Balm of the comforter
Wedge of the persuader
Bond of a marriage
Glue of a promise
Law of a contract
Directive of authority
Flowers of a lover
Healer of the hurting
Clarifier for the confused
Enlightener of the simple
Forgiver for the offended
Connector of friends
Workbench of the thinker
Bomb of the destroyer
Commander of demons
Appealers to God

The list could go on. Feel free to add. Use your own words.

They are yours to use.

"The End," Not

Of making many books there is no end, and much study wearies the body. —Ecc. 12:12b

What college student hasn't breathed this same sigh? The intriguing thing here is how early it was penned.

Exactly how many books were there way back then? It's vague, but though Hebrew was early for literacy, most of the world's languages didn't yet have an alphabet, let alone books. Even Greek was first coming into a literate form about the time of Ecclesiastes.

Reading, reading, reading, or is she dozing?

And of the few books (scrolls?) that did exist, how big were their "editions," each one laboriously hand-copied?

Compare with today, when the Library of Congress has catalogued more than 32 million books and 61 million manuscripts in 470 languages!!

And that's before Google came along and left those numbers in the Dark Ages dust!!!!!!

Still, all it takes is one book to bring on a great heaviness to the eyes and a weariness of body!!!!!!!!!!!!!!

Another intrigue about this ecclesiastical comment is how it comes at the end of its own book. Is it the writer himself who is weary? Has he made many books?

Has the compilation of this one

completely worn him out? Maybe.

The book of Ecclesiastes is one of the most unusual assemblies of thought of all time. The topics are broad, the order random, the attitude negative at worst, skeptical as a rule, often cautionary, but now and then gloriously and enthusiastically positive about living life to the fullest. It's a wide range, and it's author could have gone on and on with whatever came to his mind . . . for, as he said, there really is no end. But he finally said, "Enough."

He quit because he was tired . . . and figured you must be, too.

But he didn't quit because there would ever be an end. That's his point. There are always more thoughts, more ways to put them, more people to say them, and more people to say them to.

It's like a painting. People often ask, "How do you know when you're finished?" It can be hard to know. There's always more that can be added. Where to stop is a matter of style, and intent . . . and fatigue. Finally, it's just abandoned!

You call it "finished," and you go on to the next one.

There's always more. "The End," is only a temporary pause.

The Ultimate

Here is the whole duty of man. —Ecc. 12:13-14

Now all has been heard; here is the conclusion of the matter:
Fear God and keep his commandments, for this is the whole duty of man.

Easy: one precept. Remember that and you won't have to remember anything else. It's like we have an invisible compass, dependable for all guidance. That's pretty reassuring in the plethora of paths.

The only challenge is that the compass is invisible. It's too easy to not check it, or think it must not be working. *Fear God.* It's not an expression we use much. Instead of "fear" we

Looking ever on,
sun up, sun sets,
generations come,
generations go,
the earth remains.

like to use a lighter touch, like "profound respect." That works. But it lacks the ultimate weight of consequence.

That which we fear we generally stay away from. But in fact, the fear of an also benevolent God frees us from fear of anything else.

I scanned the headlines in today's paper . . . full of stories where no such fear exists. Rather the stories are more about the consequences.

There's a telling account in the Old Testament where Abraham traveled to a country and sensed danger. His remark to himself was, "There is no fear of God in this place" *(Gen. 20:11)*. He took measures, and those measures are part of his story. But that story is not my point, rather that a place where there is no fear of God is a dangerous place.

Why? Because there's no sense of consequence.

What we tend to forget is that "delayed consequence" is not the same as "no consequence."

Here's the rest of that final Ecclesiastes passage:

God will bring every deed into judgment,
including every hidden thing,
whether it is good or evil.

Happily, the commandments of God are not onerous. All are for our sake. Only in a few instances (maybe ten) has He had to say, "Not that." All else is ours for exploration, enjoyment, and free abandon.

And when we do blow it, He's got a solution for that, too, if we'll take it.

So finally, fear God. It's very freeing.

Loving friendship, a gift of God, everywhere around the world.

Hyatt Moore lives with his wife Anne, in Dana Point, California,
where they continue to pursue art making and life.
Their five children are all grown, scattered about the country,
nurturing their own children, and pursuits.

The Moores' art can be viewed at www.mooreandmooreart.com.

Made in the USA
Charleston, SC
25 November 2013